The Magic Is
In the Extra Mile

How to Break Free From Common Thinking

And Break Through to Your Dream-Purpose

Larry DiAngi

The Magic Is in the Extra Mile
How to Break Free From Common Thinking
and Break Through to Your Dream-Purpose
ISBN 0-9762765-1-8

Copyright © 2002 by Larry DiAngi

www. larrydiangi.com
Larry DiAngi Productions
P. O. Box 9056
Erie, PA 16505
Phone (800) 690-1372

Cover Design: D. Tucker

Text Design: Lisa Simpson

Printed in the United States of America.

Dedicated to my wife and best friend Julie.
You are a continuous inspiration to me.
Thank you for the wonderful gift of your love.

Contents

Introduction

"Most individuals desire the best possible life for themselves. Generally people do not give up and settle for less because of a lack of "wanting it". A major reason why people "miss it" is because they lack the specific steps necessary to keep their mind, will power, and emotions continually renewed in order to stay focused with enough high energy to go the distance. Your purpose for freedom in life is your birthright. You were created to enjoy abundance and freedom in every area of life. The Extra Mile does not need to be a mile of stress and backbreaking exertion. By daily practicing the reliable principles that you will find in this book, you can travel your "extra mile" with more energy, focus and momentum than in any of the preceding legs of your journey.

Taking the action needed to go to your highest level was never meant to be a struggle. If you stay "on purpose" on the inside, then the outer manifestation of your dreams will become a natural outflow of the inner focus and strength that you are developing.

If you can keep yourself right in the "real you" then your outer life will become right too!"

Larry DiAngi

Chapter
1

Going Beyond Common Miles

The purpose of a dream is to focus our attention. The mind will not reach for achievement until it has clear objectives. The magic begins when we own our dream. It is then that the switch is turned on, the current begins to flow and the power to accomplish becomes a reality.

—AUTHOR UNKNOWN

It is not so much a tragedy to be a person with no eyesight, but it is a great tragedy to have no vision.

—HELEN KELLER

There is a common way of thinking that has caused most people to live their lives on a lower level than they were created to live. Many people live and die never knowing who they really are. The misconception that some people were born to be great and that others just showed up to fulfill a destiny of struggle and lack is a falsehood that must be corrected before abundance, success, blessing or freedom can be enjoyed. If we know our true personal identity, we will have the ability to use our mind, will, emotions and physical body as the tools that they were meant to be. If we do not know our true identity then we will most likely mistakenly perceive that we are the "outer package" (the physical body, mind, will and emotions) and overlook the richness of who we really are on the inside.

Whether we live life on a higher level or stay stuck on a lower level year after year is to a great extent determined by how well we are able to keep positive control of our mind and emotions. Our willpower and physical energy are directly affected by the condition of our mind and emotions at any given moment.

We have all had the experience of finishing an important task or being involved in something that we wholeheartedly enjoy. It could be 12 midnight or 1:00 A.M., but we are still full of energy in our physical body. Our willpower is so strong that we wish we could find something else to do to put to good use the positive momentum pulsating through our being.

The flip side of this coin is also something that we are familiar with. We know what it is like to have had a full eight hours' sleep and a good breakfast and still feel sluggish. We struggle through the morning on low energy, take a break for lunch, hoping that some calories or caffeine will give us a lift but to no avail; instead, we drag through the day. If left unchecked, this downward cycle can become a weekly occurrence or even a prevailing feeling of gloom that lasts for extended periods of time. On the outside, we can appear to others to be moving right along; but on the inside, we are very aware of the fact that we are running on an empty tank.

The Benefits of Appreciating Life

Our state of mind determines our emotional state; our mental/emotional state determines the strength of our willpower and, to a great degree, our level of physical energy. Our quality of life is also experienced in direct proportion to the extent to which we keep our mind and emotions in a positive healthy state.

A national news program conducted a study of fifty people who have lived over 100 years and still lead active, happy lives. The researchers specifically looked for similarities in diet, exercise, lifestyle and habits that could contribute to their longevity and quality of life. What they found was amazing.

We are becoming more and more aware of the great benefits of a healthy diet and exercise, and the researchers expected to find these factors to be the major contributors. Through an extensive interviewing process, the news team found that some of the participants in this study had what would be considered good diets. An equal number of people were not as healthy in their food choices. Exercise and other areas of lifestyle were also not found to be a common thread throughout the group.

However, two things were overwhelmingly consistent among over 90 percent of those studied. What were these consistent traits? Nine out of ten said that throughout their entire lives they awoke every morning with an attitude of gratitude for one more day of life and that they saw each day as a precious gift. Secondly, nine out of ten stated that they felt that life was too short to hold grudges or spend time complaining, and they forgave people quickly and refused to dwell on negative thoughts.

What a revelation!

Now this is obviously not an endorsement to load up on deep-fried foods and quit exercising. We most definitely need to make sure that the foods we take into our body are good for us, and it is vitally important that we be faithful to some type of consistent physical exercise program. The point is that keeping our spirit, mind and emotions in great shape is even more of a factor in living a blessed life than anything we do or don't do physically.

Have a Mental and Emotional Advantage

The mind and emotions can be very fickle. One phone call with good news can send us through the roof with feelings that life is wonderful, the future is bright and all of our dreams will come true. Conversely, one phone call with bad news can cause us to crash through the basement floor and have to look up to see the bottom. The truth of the matter is that our ability to process what we perceive as a "good" or "bad" situation and the positive or negative resulting outlook is an automatic byproduct of our mental and emotional stability at the time.

Many people give up their hopes and dreams for a better life because of frustrations born out of a feeling that they can't sustain enough strength and momentum mentally and emotionally, which results in a lack of persistence and resolve. They really want to live life on a higher level; and, somewhere deep inside, most individuals feel that they should be enjoying a better life than they are now experiencing.

But then there are those old videotapes running in their mind that remind them of the times when they attempted to live life on a higher level and it didn't work. Mentally, they review snapshots and action footage of the times when they attempted to create a more prosperous life. They start out motivated to see greater spiritual, financial, mental, emotional and physical freedom, as well as a life filled with better loving relationships. Then they remember experiencing the frustration and disappointment of getting down the road only to hit a roadblock that has seemed insurmountable.

Though they know others who have risen above similar circumstances, they are now faced with the fact that they are too mentally and emotionally drained to go forward. Even if victory were only a few steps away, getting to the next higher level of fulfillment spiritually, financially, relationally or in any other area of life seems impossible because of their depleted mental and emotional state.

Much, if not most, of the common thinking that people buy as truth has no foundation whatsoever. The average person will check a house out thoroughly before buying it. The person will do a title search, check the basement walls for water leakage and inspect the furnace and many other things. When buying a car, this person will check on mileage, tires, engine and previous owners. But this same person will buy the average person's common way of thinking and adopt it as the absolute truth without giving it a second thought.

The only way to create real freedom is to know the truth, or "the way it really is," which includes the truth about you. You were not born to simply let life just happen to you. **You were born with a built-in creative ability to live your life totally ON PURPOSE**.

Advertising, education, Madison Avenue, Hollywood, friends, well-meaning family members, along with 1000 other influences, have hammered away at our mind, sending repeated confirming messages that tell us "You can go this high in life and not an inch higher." Then, to prove their point, people who want to keep you down or maybe just don't know any better, hold themselves up as an example, as if to say, "Do you think you are more special than we are? We're satisfied living down here, and you need to do the same."

Keep Flowing in Your Knowing

I remember years ago when I was trying to make a decision about something very important and I asked several people for their advice. The feedback I received was so different from one person to the next that I was more confused after receiving their counsel than I was before I had asked them.

I wanted to take a step in life that could bring many great benefits. I felt I should take this step forward even though it seemed very risky on the surface.

Risk is something that we have to be willing to accept if we want to go higher in life. When you know it is time to move forward, you must **take action where you are with what you have and know that the rest will fall into place as you go.** We sometimes tend to want everything to be perfect before heading for the next higher level. **Start now with what you have,** and you will be amazed at how the missing pieces will be there when you really need them.

I already knew that I was supposed to step out there and go for it but was fearful about going into unknown territory. Being faced with the possibility of a change in life is often challenging, but we seldom experience growth in any area of life without being willing to change in some way. Working this "principle of risk" is not a matter of being foolish but rather a matter of **being willing to give up what you have right now in order to go for something that you believe to be better.**

As I became more and more perplexed about stepping out on what I believed to be right, I knew that I had no guarantee of the outcome. So I decided to lay the decision aside until my mind could clear.

The next day I was speaking to a group in Houston, Texas, and the answer came to me while I was delivering my speech. I had never spoken these exact words in a speech before, and when they came out of my mouth I thought, "Larry, you need to live the words that you just spoke."

As I was making a point in my address I said, **"We must go from a place of understanding to a place of knowing; then we must keep flowing in our knowing."** When people try to discourage us or seem to contradict the next step of action that we know we need to take to flow with our purpose, we need to remember this principle: **"Never let anyone convince you that you cannot go where they have not yet been."**

The greatest way to teach principles is to see yourself as the first student who needs to hear what you are saying, and I probably needed to hear those words more than anyone else in that auditorium did.

When I took a closer look at the advice I had been receiving from various people, it became perfectly clear that the people who were fearful about the risk I was about to take had never hit the higher level that I was going for. The ones who were encouraging me to "go for it" had already hit that higher level, and some of them were five to ten levels higher than the next breakthrough I was working on. So to whom should I have listened: those who had not done it, or those who were "doing" and "being" and were further down the road of success than I was?

You see, I was being pulled off track by people's common way of thinking. Though many of them may have been well-meaning, they had no experience or authority base to draw or speak from. Overriding this common way of thinking is vital. The wonderful blessings, experiences and prosperity that are possible will come naturally when we cancel out the limiting misconceptions that we have accepted as truth.

Purpose Wins Over Procrastination

I procrastinated writing my first book for quite some time because I was waiting to learn how to use a computer. I'm not proud of the fact that I resisted getting a computer for years because I felt I was "too busy" to take the time to go through the learning curve to get started. As a fall-back strategy, I could always find someone whom I could pay to do my computer work for me.

Well, I got by just fine with those excuses until I decided to write my first book. Finally, I had a break in my speaking schedule during the time of year that I usually take off. This was the perfect time to write the book, but I still didn't know how to use a computer. To begin writing immediately would mean that I would have to do it the "hard way."

I thought, "I'll use this time off to learn how to use a computer, and then during the next extended break in my schedule I will write the book." I looked at my schedule, and the next break was in eight months. I had a decision to make: was I going to wait another year or seize the moment now, even though it meant I would have to work harder?

I knew in my heart that I was already overdue on birthing this book so I might as well get both the labor and delivery completed now or stand the risk of a miscarriage, which could feed my procrastination for several more years. I ended up writing the entire first book with pens and legal pads. Needless to say, it wasn't the easiest way to go.

Not long after that, my first book, *The Resilient Power of Purpose* (previously titled *How To Be Purpose Driven*), was released and over 120,000 copies were sold. Forty thousand more books were printed, shipped and distributed to people who had ordered copies of the book in the United States, Canada, Australia, Norway, Sweden and many other countries. In addition, I received another order for over 9000 books that went to India, Malaysia, Japan, China, South Africa and several other countries. Most recently, another order is being filled for 15,000 additional copies for Australia.

When I start adding up the numbers as the orders keep coming in, it is mind-boggling to think of how many copies of that first book will be purchased and distributed worldwide in the next several years. It's funny: after selling that many copies and receiving an avalanche of letters, phone calls, e-mails through my Web site* and encouraging statements at live events about how that book has blessed and changed lives, I have forgotten all about the hundreds of hours spent with sore fingers, pens and legal pads.

I would like to add here that I did come to grips with the fact that resisting the idea of getting up to speed with computer knowledge was something that I had to overcome. Finally, I dove in headfirst to discover the wonderful world of computers, and now there is no turning back. The computer is a part of my everyday life now, and I am always discovering

*www.larrydiangi.com

new ways to save time and be more effective and creative. I wrote this book on my laptop; and, *no,* I would not want to go back to the pens and legal pads. But at that time there were only two choices: **I had to start where I was with what I had to work with or let procrastination steal another eight months to a year out of my life.**

Who Says It's Impossible?

Some folks avoid doing anything new in their lives because they think they might be disappointed; therefore, they miss out on some of the greatest adventures. We can learn "the art" of **doubting our doubts**. In other words, instead of saying we are sure it won't work because everything is not set up perfectly, we can say, "Life is so uncertain that it is impossible to even be 100 percent sure that we will fail!" Even if things don't work as perfectly as we would have hoped for, we have learned how to "do it" and "be it" better the next time we step out.

A baby will stumble and fall many times before learning to walk, but that child has the advantage of not knowing that he or she is not walking perfectly. Therefore, that little toddler just keeps on getting up to take another step. **Sometimes there is a great blessing in not being aware of what we supposedly "can't do"; we just keep on moving forward with the belief that it is possible.**

A young man was sitting in his seventh-grade classroom on a Friday afternoon. Though there were only fifteen minutes left before he and his fellow classmates would be dismissed for the weekend, he felt nature calling him and knew that he had to act quickly. He raised his hand and asked the teacher if he might be excused to go to the restroom. With the teacher's permission and a great sense of urgency, he left the room.

Reentering the classroom, he glanced at the clock and noticed that there were only four minutes left of the school day. His eyes also immediately noticed that something new had been written on the board at the front of the room. He thought to himself, "Well, I almost got out for the weekend with no homework, but the teacher only gave us two math problems to solve and I can get those done in no time." With this optimistic outlook, he quickly wrote the two unanswered math problems in his notebook and finished writing them down as the bell rang and the rest of the class started heading for the door.

He went home and decided that he would knock out his homework after dinner so that the rest of the weekend would be free from the thought of school. As planned, he entered his bedroom after the dinner dishes were done and went straight to his desk. He sharpened a new pencil and opened his notebook anticipating a ten- to fifteen-minute mathematical challenge. Thirty minutes, forty-five minutes, one hour later, he was still working on the first problem with no success. His chair creaked as he leaned back on its back two legs, rubbed his tired eyes and thought to himself, "The teacher must have made a mistake. This math must be for an advanced class. I don't think they should give us homework this hard." Determined to get this math assignment out of the way, he plunged back in to give it another attempt. Another thirty minutes passed, and he was so mentally fatigued that he decided to go play ball with his friends and come back on Saturday morning to conquer this challenge.

The next morning after eating a quick bowl of cereal, he once again headed directly to his notebook with even greater resolve than he'd had the night before. Though it took him another forty-seven minutes, he did solve the first equation. Moving on to the second part of his homework, he again worked for another hour but could not arrive at a sensible answer. Looking at the sunny day that he was missing outside, he laid down the pencil with a commitment to return on Sunday to finish this incredibly unfair assignment. Another hour and ten minutes of rigorous effort on Sunday evening left the young man in total frustration.

Returning to school on Monday, he made his first stop a visit to his math teacher. Walking right up to the front of the room, he laid his notebook on the teacher's desk and let out a sigh. Without the slightest hint of inhibition he said, "Teacher, I worked for over two hours on the first problem of our math homework and finally figured out the answer; then I worked for hours on the second problem and still couldn't figure it out. This homework must be for a higher grade level."

The teacher interrupted this student in mid-sentence and said, "Son, you must be mistaken, I didn't give your class a homework assignment on Friday. Let me see your notebook." Looking at the two math problems, the teacher dropped his jaw in amazement. He could see that the first problem had been solved perfectly and a great attempt had been made on the second. This educator, who had thought that he had seen it all, was visibly shaken as he explained with a quivering voice to his pupil, "If I didn't see this with my own eyes I wouldn't believe it. Young man, these two problems that I wrote on the board on Friday afternoon were not a homework assignment; these are supposedly two mathematical equations that were found to be impossible to solve."

This young man hadn't known it was impossible, so he had gone ahead and done it anyway!

We have all simply scratched the surface of what is really possible for us. **We must turn on the light of the truth of who we really are and our purpose for being here. When we do this, the darkness that has blinded us and held us back will disappear, leaving in clear view the vision of the next higher level for us in life.** When you walk into a room and flip on the light switch, the darkness cannot resist the light. The brighter the light, the more the darkness is vanished.

We can arrive at this state of believing. We can live with a continual knowing that, without a doubt, we were born to live, experience and enjoy the best and then reach out and help others do the same.

People will try to discourage you when they see you going for something better than what they believe they can attain. **Many times common thinking can come disguised as common sense.** When someone tries to convince you to stay on a lower level using common thinking (disguised as common sense) as the main means of persuasion, you can just look at that person and say to yourself, **"You may think this is impossible, but I'm going to go ahead and do it anyway."**

Where do happiness, fulfillment and true abundance come from? How do you uncover and live in the strong awareness that you are living the purpose you were born for? Is it a result of a series of "lucky breaks"—being born into the right family, or by chance ending up at the right place at the right time?

All of us are born for a purpose and flourish when we are in the flow of our destiny. Just as there are animals that cannot thrive or even survive in captivity, we cannot truly experience the higher level of life that we were born to live if our mind, will, emotions and physical body are out of alignment with our personal purpose for being here.

It is amazing to watch people as they move across the stage of life. Some people are playing a part that they have rehearsed and have trained their mind, will, emotions and physical body to act out. Others are simply being who they really are and living from a strong awareness of their purpose for being here.

Realizing your dream for a life of freedom and abundance is only possible when you have decided that it is worth going the extra mile to make your dreams a reality.

Create or Stagnate

The first extra mile you will take is on the inside, and it involves changing your thoughts. We are transformed by the renewing of our mind.

The next extra mile becomes visible on the outside when your creative ability goes into action. The great things that happen on the outside are only possible because of a greater change that has taken place on the inside, in the Real You. None of us would argue with the fact that his or her physical body is a little different today than it was ten years ago, but the secret is to stay renewed on the inside on a daily basis.

When we are prospering in our purpose on the inside, outer prosperity comes along with the awareness that it already belongs to us, even before we see the outward evidence in our lives. Living your Dream-Purpose is living a life that you love to live. It is a documented fact that loving and enjoying life has a direct positive effect on your physical health.

Nothing very wonderful happens in life until you go beyond the point of no return and decide to go for the extra mile. In fact, most people are dying from boredom, living every day with the same stale thoughts that didn't work out very well for them yesterday.

The common thinking that the average person accepts as truth-reality results in the common lifestyle that you see most people experiencing on a daily basis. There is a tendency to assume that, because this common way of thinking is "the norm," it has to be based on truth. From the things we were taught by our parents in words and actions, to the thoughts and ideas that we have received from television, radio, magazines, books, education and a multitude of other influences, we can begin to accept this common thinking as "the way it really is" for us as individuals.

The corporate world has sold the line that if you're a good corporate person and you dedicate yourself to the corporate cause, then you will have security for your working years, receive a gold watch at your retirement and then live happily ever after.

We obviously have found that, even though this was accepted as "common thinking" for a period of time, the truth is just the opposite. With downsizing, rightsizing and all the other sizings taking place, people who have bought that common thinking are now finding themselves jobless at the age of forty or fifty after giving fifteen or even fifty years to a corporation. Each person "lucky" enough to keep a job after the massive restructuring of a company ends up doing his or her own job plus the jobs of two or three other people who were eliminated during the downsizing.

There is no such thing as "job security." When we get down to the way it really is, we find the only way to have real security in the area of financial income is to become strong and real in our area of expertise. Through this strength, with our value and quality of service being so high, we gain a position in the marketplace that is so solid that we gain control of our destiny. By going the extra mile that others are unwilling to go, we become "simply the best."

Those who are successful look for what they want in life; and when they can't find it, they move forward to create it. Truly successful, happy and fulfilled people are those who are willing to do all the things that others were unwilling to do.

Getting Unstuck

Throughout this book, we will remove layer by layer the limitations that result from the mistaken belief that we are small, weak and at the mercy of random circumstances. The fact that you are reading this book shows that you are hungry for principles that will help you create a greater life in the future. The true, fundamental principles of success and happiness always work if we apply them.

However, it is very common for a person to try to work principles without first of all removing the blockages that stand in one's way. As long as the barriers remain in our thinking that stop us from "knowing" these principles, the principles will only be usable to us as great concepts rather than a way of life. Here we see the difference between (1) trying to "do" the principle and (2) "being" and "living" the principle.

One such principle is included in the *law of reciprocity*. Simply stated, ***when you give, you will receive.*** If you want love, then you will have to give love. If you want a friend, then you have to give friendship. If you want more money, then you have to give some time or money. If you want time to be free to do what you enjoy doing, then you have to invest some time in a way that will purchase the free time that you desire.

Connected to this principle is the *law of use*. Simply stated, **to the extent that you flow in your purpose and use your gifts, talents and abilities, they will multiply and you will reap the benefits.** This principle, or law, working in reverse states, **If you don't use it, you'll lose it.**

Everyone has twenty-four hours in a day to work with. The major difference between success and mediocrity in any given day, week, month, year or lifetime is whether a person has been working the right principles in the right way. The person who is unaware that these principles and laws exist is very possibly going to be working them in reverse and not receiving the desired outcome.

The person who does not know that there are reliable principles and who is unaware of the law that states **as a man thinketh, so is he; and as a woman thinketh, so is she,** will become frustrated. Such a person may feel stalled, as if something is holding back progress; and, indeed, many times that is the case.

Have you ever been at a place in life where you were expending a lot of effort and to the best of your knowledge you knew that you were working the right principles and laws as strongly and consistently as you could? Yet they still didn't seem to be working and you felt stuck?

A great metaphor occurred to me one day as I was searching for a way to get out of a stuck place that I found myself in. The first part of this metaphor is to see these principles and laws as helium balloons. As we make *going the extra mile* a way of life and assimilate these principles into our heart and mind, they can lift us up to our next level. Picture these balloons attached by ropes to your arms, shoulders and back. On one balloon you see the label *"The Law of Reciprocity."* On others, you see *"The Law of Use," "Right Thoughts," "Forgiveness," "Hundred Fold Return," "Strong Work Ethics"* and so forth. Though you feel those balloons and ropes pulling on you to lift you up, you sense that something is still amiss and the process is being hindered from working properly.

You look down and immediately know why you feel stuck. Around your ankles, attached to you by chains, are a number of weights. One is shaped like an anchor; another looks like a steel ball; another appears to be a cement block; and so forth. There are labels on these weights. One is labeled *fear;* another *insecurities;* others are *unworthiness, expected failure, being born into the wrong family, not having the right connections, unforgiveness, racial and cultural limitations, physical imperfections, smallness and insignificance, unluckiness* and so forth.

The solution now becomes crystal-clear. The only thing holding you down is these weights. So what do you want to do? For people who want to live their dream-purpose, there is only one answer to this question. As you continue to read and assimilate the contents of this book, you are going to have an opportunity to do what we all need to do on a daily basis; and, of course, that is to **CLIP OFF THE WEIGHTS!**

A Little Adjustment

There are times in life when we need a major shift in our thinking to take us to the next level. At other times, a small adjustment will cause a huge positive shift in our thoughts, philosophy, reality and life experiences.

I really enjoy my car. It is loaded with just about anything you would want. The leather seats fit like a glove with added support for my back exactly where I need it. When you close the doors, you hear just a faint click. It's got power this and that and bells and whistles of every kind. Under the hood is overhead this, fuel-injected that and more power than I would ever need for normal driving.

As you can tell by my description, I don't know the exact terms that describe the features that produce the power under the hood. But I do know this: when I need to pass someone on the highway, I have to be careful not to press too hard on the gas pedal or that car will take off like a rocket.

Though normally it performs as this amazing machine which I have attempted to describe, one day I pulled out of my driveway and it sputtered a couple of times. I thought to myself, "Woah! What was that?" Out on the road, the car hesitated several more times.

I drove it straight to the dealership. The mechanic hooked it up to his computer and within a couple of minutes had diagnosed the problem. He said, "Larry, your timing is off," and I watched him take a wrench, loosen a bolt, move a bracket of some type just a fraction of an inch. Then he tightened the bolt again and said, "You're good to go."

I said, "That's it?"

He said, "Yup, that's it."

I turned the car on, and the coughing and sputtering were indeed gone; it was *purring like a lion* again!

Sometimes the slightest adjustment in our thinking is all we need to clip the last thread holding us down to the last weight in that area of our life; and, more quickly than we expect, we see that area of life take a quantum leap forward after that small adjustment. Once we experience the benefits of clipping off that weight, we move on with enthusiasm to clip the weights off our feet in other areas of our lives. All the while, we need to keep checking ourselves to make sure that the weights we clipped off in the past stay off, making sure that we don't unconsciously pick those negative ways of thinking back up again.

Out of the Comfort Zone and Into the Breakthrough

In my first book, *The Resilient Power of Purpose* (formerly titled *How To Be Purpose Driven*), I began telling the story of a very large shift that took place in my life about eleven years ago. As I speak at various conferences and conduct seminars across the United States and in other countries where my books and tapes have been distributed throughout the years, people come up to me and point to a place in my books or tell me about something I said on a tape or at a live event that really impacted them. Though it is a humbling experience, as it is for any of us, to know that we have had the privilege of helping someone along the way, it is always a highlight of my day to receive these good reports. I am often amazed at the specific parts of a book or tape that have touched and inspired someone on a deep level.

I receive many letters from people both through the mail and on e-mail through my Web site. These letters and e-mails from people from all walks of life are filled with stories of how the message that I am sharing with you through this book has enriched them. Often, what brings great inspiration and hope to me is reading or hearing other people tell about what I call the "war stories"—not wars that armies fight with guns; I'm talking about the battles that we fight in life and win.

As I speak at all types of events, for some reason people always ask me, "Can you tell us more about when you didn't have a place to live and you and Les Brown had to sleep on the office floor?" Well, here's the continuation of that story. I'll pick up where I left off in my last book.

Eleven years ago I had a headache for twenty-nine days. Aspirin wouldn't touch it. I went to doctors, and even prescription drugs didn't help. After twenty-nine days, I realized that this headache was not just a pain in my head. It was a result of the pain that was in my heart—not my physical heart; I'm talking about the fact that I was restless and very frustrated in my spirit and had been in that state of mind for quite some time.

Many years before I had made a decision that I would never stay on a lower level too long and would always go to the next higher level as soon as I knew it was time to move on. But things had gotten pretty comfortable for me. I was hosting a weekly half-hour television show on the local ABC affiliate and a five-day weekly radio program. I was also speaking locally to groups of people on a weekly basis.

I had always known that the day would come when I should break out of the local arena and go national and then global with this message. I had resisted taking that leap because I had worked so hard for what I had. This would mean starting all over again on a national scale; and if I began traveling every week, I would no longer be able to meet the time demands to continue my workload locally. The bills were being paid; and, though I had lost a lot of the passion for what I was doing, I could still produce good enough results to have it look like my heart was still in my work.

Finally, spending twenty-nine days with a headache put me in a place where I said these magic words: "I am willing to do whatever it takes to get out of this pain." By this time, I knew that I had set myself up in this sad state by not maintaining integrity with my purpose. I truly believe that if your heart is right and you are not moving along with the plan and the timetable of your purpose, then destiny will move on you to nudge you in the right direction.

Through a series of amazing happenings (which I wrote about in my first book mentioned earlier), I started working and doing seminars with Les Brown. Now this was eleven years ago; and, though many people around the world know what a great speaker and resource for selfdevelopment Les is today, back then Les was just starting out and had been traveling and speaking for about two years. He was doing very well in the speaking business, and somehow I knew in my heart that going to my next level had something to do with him and me working together.

We all need a mentor, someone who is already operating on the next higher level that we want to get to. Getting and staying in the presence of these great people is one of the keys to creating breakthroughs in our lives.

I called Les Brown's office ten to fifteen times a day for six weeks, and his staff thought I was crazy. Little did I know that after the first couple days they stopped giving him the messages. Finally, after six weeks, I talked with Les for ten minutes on a Tuesday evening. Within two weeks, I had moved from Pennsylvania to Detroit, Michigan, and Les and I had started working and doing seminars together.

Les was aware of the fact that I had "burned all my bridges" and had cut off my sources of income to make this transition. I remember Les speaking these words of wisdom to me: "Sometimes you have to give up who you are in order to become the person you want to be." I also believe that sometimes you have to give up where you are in order to go where you want to go. I had taken a big leap of faith, and that included leaving the weekly ABC television show and daily radio program to begin speaking nationally. Knowing this, Les was very kind to offer to let me stay at his house for a couple of months until I could get a place of my own.

When I first moved to Detroit, I thought, "This is great! This is going to be a piece of cake. This will be like connecting the dots to make a smooth transition into the national speaking arena." Well, how well I remember the day when I began to realize that it might not be quite that easy!

After a long day at the office, Les went home and his cousin Alexander and I went to Greek Town, a very well-policed four- or five-block area of restaurants in downtown Detroit. When I say well-policed, I mean after dark there are five to ten police officers on every block. I parked my car one block from Greek Town, which was two blocks from the downtown police station.

As we started walking the block toward these restaurants, I asked Alexander, whose nickname was "Bou," where he felt like eating and he suggested we eat at a place called Fishbones because he liked their New Orleans Cajun style of cooking. When we got to the restaurant, there was an hour wait for a table, so we decided to just head home and get some food from a drive-through on the way.

When we got back to the parking spot where I remembered parking the car, it was empty. At first I thought,

"I must be at the wrong spot"; and since we had eaten at Greek Town three times that week, I even said out loud, "Maybe this is where I parked the car last night when we came to eat dinner."

Bou was very sure that this was the spot and that the car must have been stolen. Though I didn't want to accept it, I knew he was right. We went to the police station to file a stolen vehicle report, then walked back to the office. One of the staff members gave us a ride home.

The next morning, we arrived at the office at about 8:00 A.M. I have to admit I was feeling pretty low. Here I was in a strange city with no car, and now I had to depend on other people to drive me around. This thought even crossed my mind: "Maybe this is a sign that I was supposed to stay in Pennsylvania." But in my heart I knew I was exactly where I was supposed to be.

Les said, "Larry, I have an appointment with the bank, so let's get together about 10:00 A.M. to discuss how we are going to do the seminar we have scheduled this weekend in Cleveland."

I said, "Great. I'll see you then."

As scheduled, Les arrived back at the office at 10:00 A.M. for our meeting. We went into his office and sat down. As Les swiveled around in his leather chair, I could sense that he was concerned about something. He looked at me and said, "Larry, I have to share something with you before we discuss the upcoming seminar."

I said, "Sure, Les. What's on your mind?" He continued, "Well, I just found out that some members of my staff have mismanaged my finances, and I'm going to have to let those people go. I know I'll be able to work my way out of this challenge, but one of the things that has occurred is that when they were paying my bills, they were not making my house payments. I've just found out that I have to be out of my house immediately. I know it was a real step of faith for you to move here, and I am facing some pretty big financial challenges myself due to this situation that I have just been made aware of. So the only thing I can figure out for us to do at the moment is to move out of the house and stay here in the office for a while." I said, "Okay, Les. No problem. We'll just do whatever it takes."

I have to admit that I was still numb from my car being stolen the night before, and what was happening didn't really hit me until later that night.

It was about 2:00 A.M., and Les was in his office. Bou was sleeping in his office back where the books and tapes were stored, and I was in my office. I remember staring out the window on the twenty-first floor of the Penobscot Office Building. In fact, that would be the first of many nights that I would look out of that window, gazing at the air conditioning units on the roof of the building next door, hearing them roar as they kept that building cool for the people who would leave their comfortable homes to come to work the next day.

I didn't know it at that time, but the office in which I stood would also be my bedroom for the next six months. Night after night, I would pull the cushions off the couch in the waiting room and lay them on my office floor. Now these were the same cushions that people would sit on during the day because they had made an appointment with Les or me so that we could help them become successful!

Please believe me when I tell you that *where you find yourself right now does not have to be a prediction of where*

you are going. Many, many nights I would look out of that twenty-first floor window and ask myself, "Larry, have you gone crazy? Have you lost your mind? Do you realize that you left a TV show, a radio program and all of your security and now you don't even have enough money for a place to live, your car is gone and you have to ask people for a ride? You can't go back home or people will laugh you back out of town because they told you that you were making a foolish move. You have really missed it this time."

On that office floor is where I began to learn what it takes to keep control of my mind and emotions and keep them on track even when my circumstances were screaming at me that I was a BIG LOSER.

Every night I would pray, read and go to sleep listening to motivational or inspirational teaching tapes. Les, Bou and I would take turns getting washed up in the public restroom early in the morning before the doctors and lawyers would come into their offices on the twenty-first floor. When it was my turn, I would take a portable tape player into the bathroom and listen to tapes as I was shaving and getting dressed. It took everything in me to keep holding on to the vision of my purpose and to believe that we were going to come out on top.

Many times, we would come back to the office well after midnight or even two or three o'clock in the morning after driving three or four hours from a seminar or speaking engagement and would park Les's car four levels down in an underground parking ramp. Downtown Detroit was all right during the day from nine to five when the tall office buildings and the streets were filled with the business crowd, but after dark the creepy crawlers came out—drug dealers and all kinds of other shady characters. At that time, Detroit was ranked the murder capital of the United States.

I'll tell you what: this boy from Pennsylvania learned how to run across Griswald and Woodward Avenue in record time. We would try to sneak past the security guards on the first floor because the building management had already told us that this was an office building and not an apartment complex.

Every day I worked to keep my mind and spirit in the right place. I was going out to speak at night and then making 60 to 100 phone calls per day to secure more speaking engagements. It was "nip and tuck" for six months.

Then I hit my "critical mass." Of course we know what critical mass is as it relates to atomic power, but the critica l mass that I'm talking about here is when you have put enough good into your mind and actions that all at once a great shift takes place.

One day, I made a call to a gentleman who was setting up a conference for about 2000 independent business owners. We talked about the possibility of my speaking at his event.

He asked me, "Larry, what would you speak on if you spoke at our conference?"

I said, "The title of my speech is 'Absolutely Unstoppable.'"

After a few more phone calls, he invited me to come to his event. He said, "The conference will take place next week in Reston, Virginia, and we will buy your plane ticket tomorrow and overnight it to you."

I was so relieved to hear him say that, seeing how I barely had enough money to make the payment due that week on the car I had just purchased to replace the one stolen a few months earlier.

I flew to Virginia, and the driver took me from the airport to the front of the Hyatt Regency Hotel in Reston. I walked in the hotel lobby, met the people coordinating the event and found out that a man who was one of my heroes, Charlie "Tremendous" Jones, was speaking at the same event.

I thought, "Wow! I hope I'm not out of my league here."

That night, I got up on that platform and gave it everything I had. I was talking to that group about being absolutely unstoppable. I pulled that message up from deep inside me, drawing from the personal experience that I was living through. This gave me even more passion to deliver the principles that I was sharing.

The people were clapping in response to different points I made; I could feel we were connecting in a powerful way. I saw the faces of some people in the crowd who had been frowning with their heads hung down at the beginning of my talk and who were now sitting on the edge of their seats with smiles of inspiration on their faces. It was like throwing a match on gasoline! At the end of my presentation, they gave me a roaring standing ovation that continued for such a long time that I began to blush with an overwhelming sense of gratitude for the blessing of standing where I stood at that moment.

There was a table set up in the hallway next to the auditorium where I had been given booth space to make some of my tapes available for those who wanted to purchase them. I figured I would go back to the table after I spoke to be available if a couple people wanted me to autograph some tape sets they were purchasing. When I got to the table, there were over 100 people waiting for me.

The gentleman who invited me to speak gave me an

extra $1000 above and beyond that which we had originally agreed upon. He stated that he wanted to do so because he felt that his people had received so much from my speech. I'll tell you, I was flying so high after that weekend that I almost didn't need a plane to fly back to Detroit.

One week later, I was at the office when I received a fax from a company requesting permission to distribute the tape recording of the speech "Absolutely Unstoppable," which I had just delivered. The fax said that they wanted to release it as a "standing order tape."

I thought, "They have sure been good to me. They're probably going to give the tape to maybe one or two hundred people. Sounds good to me."

The next day I received a call from this company to finalize some details about the tape distribution project and discovered that this tape was going to be sold to over 150,000 people. I just about fell out of my chair. I hung up the phone and just sat there staring at the wall thinking, "Wow! One hundred fifty thousand people are going to hear a tape of a speech that I gave at a time when I was sleeping on this office floor."

Those 150,000 tapes went out, and my phone started ringing with invitations to come and speak at large conferences. Two weeks later, I was up off the office floor and into an apartment. A quantum shift had taken place that had taken me to the next higher level of my purpose; and it's been "up, up and away" ever since. Now, every time I face challenges on my way to a higher level, I know that it is just a bit of turbulence that I must fly through on the way to a higher altitude.

If you want the best in your life, you will have to work on yourself and pay a price to keep your mind and emotions strong in the tough times. You probably won't have to sleep on an office floor to get to your next higher level and see your dreams become a reality; but, even if you do have to sleep on the floor for a while, I can tell you from experience, **IT IS WORTH IT.**

Chapter
2

Your Dream Becomes a Reality on The Uncommon Miles

Through some strange and powerful principle of "mental chemistry" which she has never divulged, nature wraps up in the impulse of strong desire, "that something" which recognizes no such word as "impossible" and accepts no such reality as failure.

—NAPOLEON HILL

If you believe it is worth it, you will be willing to look like a fool while you pursue your dream.

—WRIGHT BROTHERS

What is it that gives people the resolve to hang in there to see their dreams become a reality? Most people look similar on the outside: each one has two eyes, two legs, two arms and so forth. Yet we all have been inspired by stories of those who, even with severe physical or mental challenges, have lived their dreams. The obvious conclusion is that some people are aware of who they really are on the inside and other individuals think that the image they see when they look in the bathroom mirror is their identity. **Each of us was born for a great purpose. The real richness of who you really are is on the inside, in the Real You.**

Yes, our physical bodies are amazing. One eyeball, which is smaller than a ping pong ball, has millions of rods, which detect black and white, and millions of cones, which detect color. With over half a million nerve endings that receive messages from the rods and cones, they produce the pictures that you see instantly with amazing depth perception. Now that is a novice description of one of your eyeballs, but what about your brain, heart, circulatory system and so forth?

If the outer package is that amazing, then how incredible must the Real You be? It is impossible to exaggerate the wonder of who you are on the inside. No description in words could even begin to describe the greatness that you were created to fulfill.

It is also impossible to make the dream-purpose for your life sound more wonderful than the dream that you were born to live. You may have seen a glimpse of your greatness or a glimpse of the awesome dream-purpose you were born to live. No matter how wonderful that glimpse of the Real You was, you are better. However amazing the glimpse of your dream-purpose was, what you saw is probably just a scratch on the surface of how great your dream-purpose really is.

This is not a matter of becoming egotistical or narcissistic. In fact, the more you realize how wonderfully the Real You was created, it actually has a humbling effect on you. You begin to understand the great destiny of your purpose, and you become grateful to have been given such a wonderful gift to live.

We may all have basically the same physical organs along with other similar outer features, but there is a strength within us that cannot be revealed by a surgeon's scalpel. This invisible ingredient is the secret to being able to get to the uncommon miles, which is where our fully manifested dream-purpose-life awaits us.

When things don't seem to be going very well, and we have been consistently holding the right vision and holding the right thoughts, even if we can't explain "how" it's going to happen, we can continue to still know that we know that we know. We know that somehow all of the effort and belief and consistency that we put into our dream-purpose will pay off and the dream will be manifested in a tangible way.

When do we know it? We can only become one with our dream-purpose and truly "know it" after we have stepped over the line and gone beyond the point of no return.

An example that I have used many times in the past still illustrates this point in glaring clarity. Go with me right now to the middle of the ocean. Now see a ship crossing that ocean. Now let's go into the cabin on the top deck, where the captain and his first mate are checking to make sure that they are on course.

Just then the captain turns to his first mate and says, "Mate, we have just gone beyond the point of no return." What the captain is saying is that they have just passed the point in their voyage at which they have used up too much fuel to go back to their place of origin and only have enough fuel to get to their destination. The possibility of going back to where they have come from no longer exists, and going forward to their "purposed" destination is no longer just a good idea but has now become inevitable.

We all have that same type of point or line in our lives. Before we step over that line, we can still turn back and give up on our dream. But **once you pass that line you become a man or a woman on a mission. Quitting is no longer an option. You will not be denied. You will not settle for anything less than the highest and best that has your name on it.**

My friend, there are modern-day stories of people who have gone through even more than I did to see their dreams become a reality. We have all heard these stories, and we marvel at the courage, commitment, strength and faith of these individuals.

My story doesn't seem hard at all compared to those, but it sure brought me to a place where I knew that there were only two ways to go. While sleeping on that office floor, humbled by having to ask people for a ride because my car had been stolen, and with my credit cards over their limit and just struggling to make it through another day, I knew I had a choice to make. I would either choose to give up on my dream-purpose, fall through the bottom, get depressed and settle for a lower level; or I would have to find a way to keep moving forward even when everything around me was telling me I was a big loser. My circumstances were screaming, "Turn back now! You were a fool to think you could make this happen!"

At that time, over eleven years ago, lying on that office floor, I began to discover what thought replacement and thought exchange were all about. I began to discover how important it is to have a daily program for your thoughts and to not leave the condition of your mind and emotions open for defeat. Knowing how to keep yourself strong on the inside is more important than anything that is happening on the outside.

What is a "thought replacement and thought exchange program"? Let's move on to the next chapter in this book and we'll talk about it for a while.

Chapter
3

Thought Replacement: Renewing Your Mind and Emotions

First comes thought, then organization of thought into ideas and plans; then transformation of those plans into reality. The beginning, as you will observe, is in your imagination. Cherish your visions and your dreams, as they are the children of your soul; the blueprints of your ultimate achievements.

—NAPOLEON HILL

We are not troubled by things, but by the opinion we have of things.

—EPICTICUS

The mind and emotions are like the muscles in your physical body. With proper care and exercise, you can strengthen them. If you abuse or try to use your muscles in a way that they were not made to work, then you will hurt yourself. Lack of use and discipline to exercise your muscles will cause them to become weak.

There is a truth that, if we learn and keep it at the forefront of our minds, can save us from untold pain and misery. It is a benchmark principle pertaining to freedom from back pain. I have learned this principle the hard way, as many people have. It is simply this: *lift with your legs, not with you back.*

When you are "not thinking" and you pick up something that is only ten or twenty pounds with your body twisted off-center and using your back to lift instead of squatting down to use the muscles in your legs, you can pull a muscle and for days be plagued with back pain that will drop you to your knees. If you make this "lift with your legs, not your with back" principle "first nature" and it becomes part of your way of life, then you will automatically use your legs instead of your back as a course of habit.

Likewise, **our spiritual, mental, emotional and physical habits have either made us stronger or weaker in different areas of life.** In my first book, I gave a general overview of the Real You, the real person that you are on the inside. Now, we are going to pick up where I left off and go deeper with this *understanding*, until it becomes a *knowing*.

Your true identity, ability, strength, purpose, fulfillment and much more are on the inside of you. Every person was born with a destiny to create his or her own personal dream-purpose-life.

Perhaps you have felt better than you do right now, and you have probably felt worse at some point in your life. But the way you feel right now is not an accident. The way you feel is a byproduct of your thoughts.

The thoughts that fill our mind and the way we feel at any given moment do not have to be things that are *happening to us*. There is a difference between being a person who is taking action in life and being a person who spends more time *re*acting to people and circumstances.

The Tools That You Have Been Given

You use a hammer to pound in a nail; you use a screwdriver to screw in a screw; you use a pot to boil water; and you use the computer to do many various tasks. These are tools you use to manifest a desire that you first had on the inside. You decide that you want to tighten up a screw on a loose door handle, so you find your screwdriver and a few seconds later your desire is realized. You grip that same door handle, and now it is solid as a rock.

Our mind, will, emotions and physical body are also tools that we have been given to use.

The Outer Self
(Your Tools)

Mind

The Real You
(Your Identity)

Will

Emotions

Physical Body

Much of the confusion and pain in many people's lives is greatly due to the fact that they have a mistaken identity. They walk around every day trying to get things done to make their life better but feel so limited, trapped and stuck. For some, this can even turn into feelings of helplessness.

All the while, they mistakenly perceive themselves as only a physical body with a mind and emotions. This is like a master carpenter saying, "My talent, my skill and the creative ability I have developed over the years is in my hammer, table saw and belt sander. These tools give me my ability. If I lost my screwdriver, I would forget how to screw in a screw and have to learn how to do it all over again." That sounds pretty ridiculous, doesn't it?

The Way It Really Is

Earlier in this book, we dealt with the principle *"you will KNOW the truth, and the truth will make you free."* The fact that the truth, or "the way it really is," is available to us is a wonderful thing, but it doesn't do us any good until we know it.

Soap is available everywhere, and I am certain that even if a person could not afford to buy a bar of soap someone or some goodwill organization would give that person some free soap. But the simple fact or truth that soap is so readily available does not change the fact that there are still some dirty, stinky people around. Nobody has to have an offensive body odor, but some people do. Why? Because soap's availability doesn't do anybody any good unless that person finds some water and applies that soap to one's own body.

If you can keep your prevailing reality and your constant and continuous predominant awareness centered on the truth, then living a free life really becomes very simple.

"The truth," as it pertains to living your dream-purpose life, is simply this: the way it really is, the way life is really supposed to be, who you really are on the inside and who you were created to be.

We are transformed by the renewing of our mind; and as one thinketh, so one will be. The key here is being able to maintain the right "day and night," continual consistency.

The challenge for most people is that they are not aware of what they are thinking on a minute-by-minute, hour-byhour and day-by-day basis. They are even less aware of "the thoughts they have about their thoughts"; in other words, the "*opinions* they have about their thoughts."

The opinions we have about our thoughts can make all the difference. Two people can be put in the same exact situation, and for one person it may strike fear in the heart and for another it may stir up courage or even positive anticipation. The distinction is simply the different perceptions of the situation, and those perceptions are created by opinions not necessarily having anything to do with the actual facts about that particular circumstance.

Later in this book, we will look at a system I have developed to ensure that we stay aware of what we are thinking on a minute-by-minute, hour-by-hour and day-by-day basis. In Chapter 6, I will give you an outline for a "Daily Thought Replacement Program" that you can use to create your own personal daily strategy for monitoring and exchanging your thoughts.

It Works—If You Work It

Here are a couple of letters from the many letters and emails that my office and I receive continuously concerning the overwhelming effectiveness of the program that I will share with you in Chapter 6. I am not giving you these letters to tempt you to skip to Chapter 6 now. In fact, I would advise against doing that because you will receive much more from the outline of the program if you first assimilate the information in the next few chapters. The reason I want to include these letters is to "whet your appetite" and to let you know that a concrete and practical strategy is on the way to you as you continue to read the following pages.

Dear Larry,

...I heard you speak at a conference in Reno, Nevada, and bought your books and tapes. Since then, I have started working the daily program that you teach. The morning and evening times of thought replacement have changed my life. I do not begin my day without telling myself, I was born to succeed; I am worthy of my dream." Then, all throughout my day, I continually keep my thoughts more and more on target. I cannot fully put into words how this has changed how I feel, talk and even act. People ask me, "What happened to you? You seem so much more positive and optimistic." Well, that is how I am now. I know that I will live my dream and that I settled long enough for the "lower level" that you talk about. I have determined to go to my next level—and as soon as possible. I have been working the daily program for three weeks, and I know there is no turning back. I know my thoughts have held me back in the past, and now I am replacing them with thoughts that are setting me free to see a whole new world and future....

With sincere gratitude,

J. M.
Long Beach, California

Hi, Larry,

...I especially want to express a "thank you" for bringing the principles you teach to the forefront for me. I was looking for a daily formula to keep me on track; I seem to be up and down. I feel very sure one day and then have trouble the next holding the right vision that you wrote about in your book. I have read many self-development books and listened to a lot of tapes and attended seminars whenever possible. But the one thing that I missed, and I am so glad that you made clear to me, is that I needed the consistency of working on myself and my thoughts...daily. If a person does not have a deliberate program like the one you teach, they will inevitably miss a lot of days and a lot of life. I have also noticed that I am not as susceptible to negative people now. I feel less of a need to spend time with those ten-minute, two-minute and thirty-second people that you talk about.

On the business side, I have passed a milestone this month that is amazing. I have been in business for twelve years and never have been able to do 1000 points in one month. This month I did close to 2000 points, and the month isn't over. I am sure, without a doubt, that it is a direct result of using the daily program that you have taught me through your books and tapes. Daily my thoughts are stronger, and I know that is why my life is also becoming stronger and more purpose-driven towards my dream every day.

Keep up the good work and may you be richly blessed,

D. G.
Toledo, Ohio

Your Belief Creates Your Reality

Most folks go through life unconscious of the fact that they are even thinking thoughts. They are not concerned whether these thoughts, which are creating their particular reality in life, are true or false.

Thoughts are powerful. You see, feelings of insecurity, inferiority, fear, doubt, security, strong positive selfesteem, love and faith are born out of our thoughts. But the tricky part of this is to make sure that we are operating in the right reality.

Let me give you an example that illustrate this point. See yourself on a beautiful back road somewhere high up in the mountains. You have been driving for hours and decide to stop at a little country store to get gas and a snack. After you fill your gas tank, get your snack and pay the cashier, you walk back to the car, take one look at the front seat and say to yourself, "I've been driving for six hours. I need to stretch my legs before getting back behind that wheel." You notice a path going into the woods, so you walk back into the store and ask the person behind the counter, "Where does that path lead?"

The cashier replies, "That is a nature trail. It is beautiful to see the leaves changing color this time of year." You answer, "Would it be okay if I took a walk down your trail? I need to stretch my legs before continuing my trip."

"Sure," says the cashier. "Feel free to do that, but keep your eyes open. There's really nothing to worry about, but just remember this is bear country."

Now, see yourself starting to walk down the path in this beautiful, densely wooded forest. Hear the wind rustling through the tops of the trees; smell the distinct sent of the foliage and wildflowers growing along the path. You've been walking about five minutes, and you notice that the path you are walking on intersects with another path.

Just as you finish making this observation, all of a sudden you hear a tremendous shaking of a bunch of thick bushes behind you. You see a big patch of something brown and fuzzy, and it moves out and then back into the middle of the bushes. Then you hear a deep growl.

On impulse, remembering that the cashier told you to keep your eyes open in the woods because you are in "bear country," you begin to run down the path. Your heart feels like it will beat out of your chest; you feel cold and clammy; you are sweating profusely. You duck down, barely missing a low hanging branch. Then you continue to run as fast as you can for about four or five minutes.

Once you finally stop, you stand there panting uncontrollably and you realize that the part of the path you were on must have been made in a circle because you are right back at the place where the two paths intersected. You are sure that the bear must have moved on by now.

You look closer at what you thought was a piece of brown fur and see that it was really some brownish-colored moss on the tree behind the bushes. You hear some tiny squealing sounds coming from the bushes; but you know that this sound could only come from a little animal, so you spread the bushes to take a peek.

There before you is the cutest litter of puppies you have ever seen. Just then you look a couple of yards to the left and you see the puppies' mother. She doesn't move or even give you any sign that she wants to move, but she does look you right in the eye and give you a very deep growl, as if to say, "You'd better not get any closer to my babies or you will be in big trouble."

With a smile on your face, you start walking back to your car thinking to yourself, "Wow! My mind can sure play tricks on me!"

Obviously, there never was a bear to run from; you just *thought* there was. Now ponder this question. Would the sensations in your physical body or the terror in your mind have been any different if the bear had actually been there? No. Whether the bear was really there or not wasn't the issue. You thought the bear was there, and that was enough to create the experience of running in fear while believing you were in serious physical danger.

Most of the fears that stop a person from making one's dream a reality are not caused by a real threat.

Similarly, we know that scientific medical studies have been conducted in which people experiencing physical symptoms were given "placebos," pills containing nothing more than sugar or some other substance that in no way would ever affect their symptoms for the positive or the negative. Yet when these test patients were given these pills, they were told that they contained very effective medicine to relieve their suffering or cure their illnesses. In many cases, the symptoms completely disappeared even though there was no medicine in the pill.

Why? Because the patients believed the word of the person who told them that by taking this little pill, they would be cured. The words of promise spoken to them by that person who they perceived to be an expert and authority in curing their illness became a collection of thoughts that became rooted deep in their heart and mind. Then that collection of thoughts became their philosophy for getting well. As they meditated on this accepted philosophy and continued to reinforce it by taking the action of using the pills as directed, over a period of time their philosophy turned into their reality. Once their heart and mind were saturated *day and night* with this reality, they reached *critical mass* and the built-in healing and restoration process went to work in their physical body to correct the problem. Whether it was a physical ailment or simply psycho-somatic.

In like fashion, when you replace thoughts of failure, lack and insecurity with true thoughts and become absolutely convinced that your true destiny is to *prosper* in everything that you do, then your philosophy changes completely. Do you realize that the common thinking of the majority of people is permeated with the belief that a dream-life is only possible for a select few? The truth is that it is possible for anyone who really believes it is available and is willing to go into massive action to realize one's dream for freedom in every area of life.

Therefore, the reality that many people have accepted is a complete lie. Now I know it is pretty strong to describe the common thinking of many people as a "lie," but think about it for a moment. Why is it that those who have (1) set goals, (2) written those goals down on a piece of paper, (3) spoken those goals out loud to themselves and to a small group of like-minded partners and (4) reviewed and expanded on those goals several times per day, have the same consistent results? These people have been irrefutably proven to be 95 percent more likely to achieve the goals they have purposed to accomplish; they have engaged their "ear gate," their "eye gate" and their "mouth gate" to receive and give only thoughts that are congruent with their desired outcome.

We have locks on the doors of our houses. When we drive through a neighborhood that looks dangerous, we make sure that our car doors are locked. When someone knocks on our hotel room door, we look through the peephole to see who it is before opening the door. Yet it is very common for people to have no discipline when it comes to protecting their mind or choosing their thoughts carefully and deliberately.

We can control what comes out of our "mouth gate." Though we can't always control what we see, we can control what we decide to look at and what we will spend concentrated times on letting into our "eye gate." We can't control everything that our ears hear, but we can decide what we will really listen to and allow in our "ear gate" and hear with our heart.

For example, imagine someone walks up to you right now and asks you, "What is your name?" You respond by pronouncing your name in a clear, strong voice. Next, the person asks you to spell your name. You respond by spelling your name slowly and with perfect articulation. Immediately, the person both pronounces and spells your name back to you with perfection.

After this, the person looks you right in the eye and says, "That is not your name. You must be mistaken." You then reassure the person that in fact this is your name and pull out your driver's license to show your name, which is printed clearly. The person responds, "You may think that is your name, but it must be a misprint."

How much success would anyone have in convincing you that your name is really not your name? You would just look at that person and wonder if he or she were mentally sound.

You see, your thoughts, philosophy and reality about your name are set and are unaffected by this challenger. When you *see* your name on a piece of paper, there is no doubt that that is your name. When you speak your name, you never question it. When you hear your name spoken, you immediately, without hesitation, know that the name being spoken belongs to you.

We can get to know our dream-purpose just as well as we know our name! *Understanding* something is good; but when we come to a place of *knowing*, the resilient power of our purpose kicks in.

Someone may say, "Okay, Larry, enough about this knowing stuff. I can see my circumstances, and there is no way that I could ever go higher in life. So all this knowing stuff must be for somebody else."

A person who would say this has actually already decided what he or she knows. This person is already using the power of knowing in reverse and is really saying, "I *know* that I can't *know* anything better." This individual knower apparatus is working perfectly. The person has been using the eyes, ears and mouth to establish reality on a lower level.

Years ago in the "horse and buggy days," there was a man who traveled by horseback all day and finally reached his destination, which was a town named Smithport. He found the only motel in the little town and checked in at the front desk. Arriving at his room, he was so tired that he didn't even unpack his bag or undress; he just kicked off his boots and fell right into bed.

It was a hot, humid, summer night, and after he had lain there for a few minutes he noticed that the air in the room was stale and even hotter than the temperature outside. So he got up in the pitch-black darkness, felt his way over to the window and attempted to open it; but it wouldn't budge. He felt along the bottom of the glass pane and perceived that it must have been painted and the paint had sealed the window in a closed position.

He was so tired and so hot that he decided that he would break the window and in the morning pay the motel owner to have it replaced. He picked up his boot, and with one swing the glass shattered, leaving only small, sharp pieces of glass around the edges. Though he could not see it because of the blackness of that starless night, he leaned over to where he assumed the opening was and took in a deep breath, saying to himself, "Aaah, that's better."

With that he lay back down, fell right to sleep and slept all night. When he awoke in the morning light, he rubbed his eyes; and, as he stretched his arms and gazed across the room, he couldn't believe his eyes. In the midst of the total darkness of the previous night, he hadn't broke the glass out of the window; in fact, there wasn't even a window in the room. All he had done was break a perfectly good piece of glass out of the door of a bookcase sitting across the room!

There had been no additional fresh air coming into that room the night before, but he had *thought* there was; and that had enabled him to get a good night's sleep! **The quality of our thoughts determines the quality of our life.**

I have mentioned this before, but it definitely bares repeating: through research, psychologists and psychiatrists have found that 87 percent of the average person's self-talk is negative. On a daily basis, a person thinks between 40,000 to 50,000 thoughts each day; that is between 34,800 and 43,500 negative, debilitating thoughts per day.

That means the average person is only experiencing 13 percent of the possible dream-life he or she was born to live. Why 13 percent? Because that is the total of the average person's positive self-talk which comes from the total of one's true, reality-based thoughts.

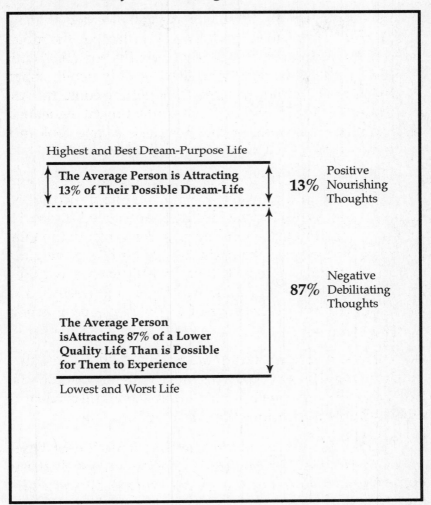

The average person is literally attracting 87 percent of what the individual doesn't want. Thoughts are things; thoughts are decrees; and with thoughts, we put in our order for what we will receive in life.

You may have ordered a pizza to be delivered to your

house, and when it got there it had different toppings than you had ordered. You may have asked someone to get you a pen, and the person came back with a pencil. But don't worry about that happening with the *"thought principle."* You can write it down and take it to the "bank of the way it really is": *"As you think, so you will be."*

Thought Replacement

So what is *thought replacement?* It is simply turning on the light of truth-based reality and removing the darkness of falsity-based reality.

Someone may ask, "If it's false or erroneous, then how can it be reality? What we have come to understand is that if you believed that the bear was really chasing you, then that is "real for you" and that will be your brief life experience at that moment. This does not mean that it is a fact or that it is real when you compare it with the truth.

Have you ever heard these phrases: "the earth is flat" and "this airplane invention won't work; if God had meant man to fly, then he would have given him wings"? At one time, these were well-accepted by the masses as total truth—until they were proven to be false.

So what we need to do continually is work on *thought replacement*, which is simply exchanging those false thoughts for the thoughts that are in alignment with the principles of purpose, life, success, happiness and fulfillment. How to do this on a daily basis will be something that I will explain in the future pages of this book.

There is no way to accomplish this without being on a daily quest and maintaining continuous focus on a consistent basis.

We understand what negative self-talk is. For example, it is what sometimes happens when you are thinking about, planning for or acting on the realization of your dreams in life. At times there is a chitter-chatter in the back of your head saying: "You can't do that." "You're not smart [or rich or talented or good-looking] enough." "Nobody else in your family is successful; who do you think you are—some kind of big shot?" Or, "Yes, the rest of your family is successful but they have all the brains and talent; when you were created, there wasn't enough left for you." "You don't have the right connections." "Sure, someone else could enjoy a dream like you are thinking about, but people like that are different; they're special." And this chatter goes on and on and on.

How to Get Rid of Stinking Thinking

Common thinking can cause us to become totally immersed in negative self-talk without even being conscious that the chitter-chatter is there. So the first necessary step is to become aware that some of the dialog going on in your brain is actually working against you. This is more than just recognizing that some of your self-talk is negative. Realizing that it is happening gives you the conscious opportunity to do something about it.

We can take one of two approaches to remove negative self-talk. We can either (1) do extensive research on all the intricate details about how dark and damaging our particular false self-language is or (2) we can concentrate on filling ourselves with positive, truth- and purpose-based selftalk and let the positive flush out the false.

The second is obviously the better choice. You can correct your thoughts by becoming so disgusted with them that you will finally take action to find a better way of thinking, but the main problem with this approach is that you spend way too much time thinking about what's wrong. By the time you have corrected that particular area of negative self-talk you were working on, spending so much time wading around in all that garbage, you could have actually strengthened self-doubt in another area of your thought life.

Another way to look at this whole idea of aligning our thoughts with the right principles and removing the negative self-talk is to become conscious of the constant "videolike footage" and series of "snapshot-like pictures" being shown in our mind.

We have a recall that is like video clips running in our head. From our childhood to the present day, we access and play back these video clips for a review when specific situations or certain people remind us of a similar circumstance or feeling that matches the experience that we have had. This video-type footage is stored in our mind our entire life. Some of this footage has a positive, reassuring effect on us, and some of it causes us to doubt or be assaulted by fear.

There are also still-frame snapshot-like pictures that we automatically access and put up on the projector screen of our mind that have a similar effect on us.

As we replace the negative self-talk with positive, true, principle-based thoughts, we are at the same time reducing, and can even void out the effect of, the debilitating video and snapshot-like pictures that have limited our perception in the past. In fact, the beautiful thing that starts t o happen is that when we are presented with a particular circumstance, our mind and heart will do the standard rundown of all of the video footage and snapshot information that we have stored over the years. Instead of pulling up something negative and debilitating for us to watch, our mind will automatically bypass the old footage or snapshots it used to be prone to access. Instead, it will pull up different pictures and action footage that are in alignment with the new true, principle-based thoughts we have been meditating on. The old debilitating footage and pictures will simply begin to collect dust; and as we continue to practice thought replacement, they can even end up in the "recycle bin" or be erased completely.

Some people take great pride in how many movies they have in their video library, usually stored in a visible display case somewhere near their television entertainment center. Others are forever pulling out the picture albums from weddings, vacations and the like. Though a certain amount of enjoyment can be derived from this type of activity, the more important thing to work on is to make sure that you are watching the right movies and looking at the right pictures *in your mind*. Bringing in good, new, strengthening thoughts and flushing out the old, debilitating, weakening ones is a big part of being free to live the wonderful dream-purpose life that you we born to know as "your reality."

In your experience, when you have walked into a room and flipped on the light switch and the lights have come on, have you ever known the darkness to argue with the light? The darkness can't put its hands on its hips and say, "I may have left last time, but this time I'm staying." No. When you flip the switch and the lights come on, the darkness has to leave. The more wattage you have in the light bulbs, the quicker and more completely the room will be filled with light.

The same principle applies to *thought replacement*: the rate and degree of completeness at which you bring in the right thoughts will be the same rate and degree of completeness at which the false thoughts are forced out.

There is no quick fix or instant mental drain cleaner that can circumvent the necessity for this daily approach.

It is always thrilling for me to see people who are hungry to implement the thought replacement program in their lives. One day after I finished speaking at a business conference, a lady came up to my book and tape table and said, "Thank you so much for sharing your message with us tonight. I want to buy all of your tape programs and books. Give me one of each. I want to take these materials home and digest these principles to renew my thoughts."

As I was autographing one of her books, she shared with me how she had really been struggling with negative self-talk in her personal and professional life and that she knew the books and tapes would help her immensely. Then she spoke a sentence that I will always remember: *"You know, Larry, life would be really easy if it weren't so daily!"*

Struck with the glaring reality that filled the words that had just come out of her mouth, I looked at her and said, "Wow! That is a profound statement!"

I think she was onto something there; and since life is so "daily," only a daily approach to keeping our thoughts right will get the job done.

Each day we must keep the inside positive pressure greater than the outside negative pressure, as illustrated in the diagrams below. As we feed on the right thoughts, we build up a resource of positive inner strength. Negative pressure is coming at us constantly from people, media, political struggles, family problems and a variety of different influences. **If you keep your inner positive**

pressure greater than the negative outer pressure, then you will not cave in under the weight of daily life or the doubts that come to steal your dreams.

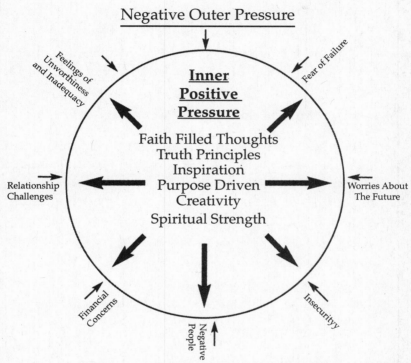

As we receive, assimilate and know more principle- and truth-based reality thoughts, we are automatically reducing and pushing out cancelled-out negative thoughts. Since the average person's negative self-talk is at 87 percent, then we need to begin reducing that number. For example, we should go from 87 to 80 percent; from 75 to 50 percent; 40 to 30 percent; 20 to 10 percent; and of course, the objective is to get the negative self-talk thoughts down to 0 percent in each individual area and in our thought life as a whole.

We may never get to 0 percent negative self-talk in all of the different areas of our life at one time. But, even if someone goes from 87 percent to 40 percent, that person will still experience a dramatic life-shift and change for the better and be on the way to his or her best. As you go through what is necessary to replace and change your thoughts, you will reach a point where you will notice outward evidence that you are living a blessed life. People around you will say, "What's up with you? You seem different. Did you win the lottery or something? You seem so much better now than the last time I saw you."

Learning, Unlearning and Learning Again

I remember a man named Bill, whom I knew quite well several years ago. Whenever I would have a speaking engagement in the city in which he lived, he was sure to be in the audience. After I was done with my presentation, I would immediately see him coming towards me to say hello; he would be working as hard as he could to get to me as quickly as possible.

The reason that Bill had to work so hard is that he has muscular sclerosis. His legs are bent and twisted, his back is arched and his arms and hands are curled up in front of him. When he would come up to me to say hello, many times he would have a cassette tape in his hand.

I remember watching him making his way to where I was sitting autographing books. I wanted to get up and go to meet him halfway so that he wouldn't have to work so hard. Obviously, I couldn't do that because it would have been very rude to just get up abruptly and leave the people who were talking to me at that moment.

With sweat dripping down his face, and out of breath, he would finally arrive where I was sitting. With slurred speech, and using all of his concentration to form his words, he would greet me; I would stand up, and we would give each other a firm handshake. After this, Bill would usually hand me his tape and say, "Larry, this is the latest speech I gave recently; I hope you enjoy it." Then we would talk for a while.

You see, Bill is a very powerful public speaker, not because he is such a great orator but because he is the message that he is sharing. One day he told me his story, which was very heartwarming and quite moving. He had been unable to walk and was living the life of a reclusive handicapped person. Then he started attending seminars to improve his life and began reading books and listening to tapes on the same subjects. Over a period of time, Bill worked on himself on the inside and changed his thoughts to the point that he was able to walk, and he could talk 80 percent better than before. Then he started to go out and tell his story to groups of people. Newspapers even featured articles about him and television programs told special interest stories about him.

During one of the conversations that Bill, another friend and I were having, I asked Bill, "How did you start to walk and improve your speaking so much in such a short amount of time?"

Bill's answer was a revelation: "Larry, when I started spending less time with other handicapped people and more time around people who walk well and talk clearly, I began to discover that I had learned much of my disability from other disabled people. When I began seeing close-up examples of people living normal lives, I gave it a try; I learned to walk, and my speech has improved dramatically."

Wow! How many of the restrictions and limitations that we take for granted are really just false handicaps that we learned and can also unlearn and replace with the greatness that we've had locked up inside of us all along?

For the average person, 87 percent of life is filled with learned restrictions. The average person would not read this book, so the fact that you are interested in the information contained in this book would indicate that your negative self-talk is lower than 87 percent.

It would be very complex to come up with what one's exact percentages of true-positive or false-negative thoughts are; but whatever the percentages are, one thing is for sure: no one on this planet has even scratched the surface of one's true potential.

The greatest minds that have ever lived were and are considered geniuses. We are told that the most creative people on earth and those who have made the greatest breakthroughs in science, medicine and physics have probably still only used less than 10 percent of their brain to do what they have done and be who they have been. Maybe the other 90 percent of our brain is waiting for something good to work with and cannot operate on negative self-talk!

Can your life change for the better? YES. Can you create a breakthrough in every area of your life? YES. Can you see your dream-purpose become a reality? YES. Plant a thought, and you will reap an act; plant an act, and you will reap a habit; plant that habit, and you will reap your lifestyle; plant your lifestyle, and you will reap your destiny.

Chapter
4

Critical Mass Creates Freedom

Two frogs fell into a can of milk,
Or so I've heard it told;
The sides of the can were shiny and steep
The milk was deep and cold.
"Oh, what's the use?" croaked Number One,
"'Tis fate; no help's around.
"Goodbye, my friend! Goodbye, sad world!"
And weeping still he drowned.
But Number two, of sterner stuff,
Dog paddled in surprise,
The while he wiped his milky face and dried his milky eyes.
"I'll swim a while at least," he said—
Or so I've heard he said.
"It really wouldn't help the world if one more frog was dead."
An hour or two he kicked and swam,
Not once he stopped to mutter,
Then hopped out, via butter!

—T. C. HAMLET

Freedom never comes cheap and never goes on sale. You must pay full price, but it is always more than worth it. Whatever you have dreamed that freedom is, it's always better than you imagined!

—LARRY DiANGI

I touched on this point very briefly earlier in this book, but now let's take a closer look at this principle. We have all heard about the atomic bomb and also the use of nuclear energy. *Critical mass* is a nuclear term. It refers to the minimum amount of radioactive material that will cause a nuclear reaction.

We also see this same type of principle at work with one of those old-fashioned scales, such as the scale used as a symbol of justice. I'm sure you have seen one of these scales at some point in your life. You can use this type of scale by putting a metal weight that weighs a specific amount—let's say three pounds—on the left side of the scale and then filling the other side of the scale with whatever substance or material you want to weigh. Let's say you want three pounds of coffee. You keep putting coffee beans on the right side of the scale until it drops down to be exactly level with the left side with the three-pound weight. Now you know that you have three pounds of coffee. Though it takes hundreds of coffee beans to bring the scale level, once it's level and filled to the three-pound point, it will just take a small amount of additional coffee beans to "tip the scale" all the way to the right side.

You can also compare increasing your percentage of positive, principle-based thoughts to how nuclear power is released. We call it nuclear power because the power is trapped in the nucleus of the atom until the right principle is used to release it. A negative electron cloud surrounds the nucleus of the atom, which is very strong. A neutron beam must be used to break through the electron cloud and penetrate the nucleus. The neutron beam must continue to bombard the electron cloud until it breaks through to reach the nucleus and then continues to bombard the nucleus of the atom until it splits. From this comes a chain reaction and a massive release of energy.

This is the same type of process we go through to see our dream-purpose become a reality. **You may dream of greater freedom in the different areas of your life. You were created to enjoy freedom of every kind, including spiritual, mental, emotional, financial, relational and much, much more—freedom in your willpower, freedom from the fears that have held you back from your highest good and freedom from the "fear of people."**

How many of our actions are controlled by our desire to please other people, even when pleasing them denies us the pursuit of our dreams? What could you accomplish if you no longer needed other people's approval in order to feel better about yourself? What if you were so filled with the right thoughts that people could adamantly disagree with you and even oppose you but it still wouldn't sway you from what you know that you know that you know?

Freedom is a wonderful thing. Of course, the real challenge is to keep on believing in and going for greater amounts of freedom even at times when your circumstances are telling you that you are going to stay stuck forever.

The Darkest Hour Is Right Before the Dawn

In the releasing of nuclear power, another very interesting phenomenon occurs that is directly paralleled with the breakthrough process necessary to make your dreams a reality. Right before the atom splits, the nucleus actually depresses, and for a short time it seems that the energy it took to penetrate the negative electron cloud to reach the nucleus was expended in vain. Then all at once, while still in a depressed state, the nucleus undergoes a total change. The atom splits, incredible energy is released and a chain reaction occurs, affecting the surrounding atoms. Likewise, **at the point when it seems that you have wasted months or even years pursuing a dream, many times a few more hits at it is all it will take to break things wide open.**

I think back to my own experience sleeping on that office floor. What if I would have stopped one phone call short? What if I hadn't dialed the phone to call that wonderful gentleman who invited me to go speak in Reston, Virginia, which also resulted in 150,000 of my tapes being distributed? What if, a week or even a day before, I would have become so beaten down and discouraged that I would have simply given up taking any further action on my dream-purpose?

I shutter to think of what I would have missed. In the past eleven years, this has also resulted in a multitude of speaking engagements, with thousands of people present at each. I have had the privilege of speaking live to hundreds of thousands of people as a chain reaction from that one presentation titled "Absolutely Unstoppable." Yes, we must be absolutely unstoppable to see our dreams become a reality. The only way to have and sustain this kind of an unstoppable spirit is to ignite it and then continue to fuel it with the right thoughts.

The One Thought That Tips the Scales in Your Favor

Critical mass, as it pertains to our thoughts, is the minimum number of thoughts it takes to cause a chain reaction in our life. This works in forward motion for the positive or in reverse for the negative, as most principles do.

Principles used properly will cause an outward release of positive results. Principles used improperly will cause negative outward results and will implode on the person misusing them.

How many principle- and truth-based thoughts does it take before a person is prepared for an act of heroism? How many thoughts does it take for a person to know one was born to be a success?

We all know that a man and a woman having a baby together does not necessarily make them good parents. How many thoughts does it take for a woman or a man to become a loving, nurturing parent?

Since it is impossible to calculate how many thoughts it will take, we need to follow the pattern that has worked for every other person who has made one's dream a reality. The only guaranteed method and strategic approach is to be on a constant daily quest. Someone once said, **"The only way to accomplish great things is to think about them all the time and take continual proactive action on your thoughts."**

We all know what temporary motivation is. We can get motivated one minute, and an hour later it's gone. It's like our motivation evaporated into the air like steam from a teapot.

Motivation occurs in our mind, will, emotions and physical body, which compose our "outer self." I have asked people when I speak from the platform, "How many people here would like to never have to try to get motivated again, but be able to stay motivated all the time?" Invariably, just about every person in the crowd raises a hand immediately.

Then I show them exactly how to do that. Instead of going for outer *motivation*, you begin to do what is necessary to stay constantly *inspired* on the inside.

You see, motivation is a byproduct and not something that stays alive in and of itself. That's why outer motivation, at its best, is only temporary. As we practice constant and continual thought replacement and fill ourselves with more and more inspiring, faith-filled thoughts, we will stay inspired on the inside and the outer motivation will come naturally and will not fade.

Don't Go to the Ocean With a Thimble

I have three daughters and one son: fifteen-year-old Damica, twelve-year-old twin girls, Dina and Denee, and eight-year-old Anthony. Throughout the years, they have used many different strategies to negotiate with me when they have had a specific objective in mind.

One of the most effective of these various techniques is pretty obvious to me now, and I must admit that it is still one of my favorites. Every once in a while I see them having a meeting, and I have come to know what is about to happen when one of these deliberations is taking place. I have overheard the discussions in their little conferences when they were totally unaware that I was within earshot. These little sibling consultations are usually based on one topic and have one objective. The focus revolves around one basic question: "How do we get Dad to stop at the store and buy us a cappuccino and a few other tasty treats?" Well, I know that their meeting is over when I see one of them leave the huddle and begin to approach me. I also know that sometime during their little planning session the approaching negotiator has been chosen as their current liaison, sent forth to achieve their collective goal.

A particular time that first comes to mind is one of many in which Denee was the chosen delegate. I was sitting in a chair reading, and after I overheard the short meeting I saw Denee approaching me. She came over and sat on my leg and put her arm around my neck. Her first words were brief and well-chosen. "Dad," she said, "can we go to the store and get a cappuccino and maybe one other treat?"

I didn't say yes right away because I have learned that if I hold out for a few minutes, certain perks will follow my hesitation. If I resist the temptation to say yes immediately, I know that I will get hugs, kisses and possibly some promises of good future behavior and other similar fringe benefits.

I said, "Well, honey, maybe we can do that."

With that, Denee shifted into a mode of accelerated negotiating strategy. "Please, Dad," she said.

I could almost hear the wheels turning in her head as she tried to choose her next step carefully. The approach she chose was to try to make me feel as if I would be remiss to not say yes to her request. "Daddy," she said (you will notice that she now addressed me as "Daddy" instead of "Dad" to build a greater level of rapport).

After successfully crowning me with the title of "Daddy," which I do have to admit pulls pretty hard on my heartstrings, she continued: "It has been a long time since we stopped for a cappuccino. In fact, we were going to stop and do this a few days ago and we were late and didn't have time."

Then she put the icing on the cake. I think she and her other collaborators know that the next step in this particular negotiation strategy will work every time if it follows an effective series of convincing pleas. Denee then gave me a big kiss on the cheek. "Please, Daddy," she said in her cutest, most lovable voice, and then put her head on my shoulder.

Well, you know as well as I do that it was all over. It was a "done deal." I said, "Okay, honey, we have to go out in about an hour. We can stop and you all can get a cappuccino and one pack of sugarless gum. How does that sound?"

"Great!" Denee exclaimed. With her request being granted, she then jumped off my lap to go share her victory with her cohorts.

I remember sitting and pondering an amazing thought after she left: "Wow! That was a really big deal for her—a ninety-nine-cent cup of cappuccino and a sixty-nine-cent pack of gum. If she only knew what I would do for her and my other children if they really needed it! If their life depended on it and they had a critical need, I would spend every penny I have and then mortgage myself to the hilt to save them from harm."

There was no way that they could comprehend at that point in their lives how strong and inexhaustible their daddy's love is for them. The collection of their thoughts about my love and commitment to and for them was still limited. They knew they could get stuff from Dad, and I know they truly love me; but all of the deeper thoughts and principles about love had not yet been registered in their minds to form a complete philosophy and reality about my love for and commitment to them. Over time, their collection of thoughts will grow and, therefore, they will also gain a fuller awareness of how my heart wants them to be blessed in every way.

We can live with the same perception that Denee had. It's kind of like going to the ocean with a thimble to get water! The purpose that you have in your sphere of activity is just as great as anyone else's purpose in that person's sphere of influence. So, instead of going to the ocean with a thimble, let's work on our thoughts until we can at least see ourselves pulling up to the ocean with a fleet of semi-tanker trucks!

Right On...

What if you were laser-focused on your dream-purpose to the point that it became your predominant world of reality and you knew that everything else in life was simply given to you to help facilitate your purpose? What we're talking about here is being *on* instead of *off*, *flowing* instead of *struggling*, *attracting* instead of just trying to *get* stuff, *acting* instead of living your whole life simply *reacting* to people and circumstances. Begin to *be* "who you really are" instead of just *doing* a lot of things to try to feel like you are being somebody special. What an amazing difference there is between these options!

We all know what it's like to be "on a roll" for a short period of time and everything we touch seems to turn out great. At times like this, we may even do or say something that is so amazing that we have to step back for a moment and say to ourselves "Woah! That's pretty good! Did I do that?" This experience is similar to when the dancer becomes one with the dance, the musician becomes one with the instrument or the baseball player becomes one with the bat: both move seamlessly together.

I played drums in rock bands in my earlier years, and I distinctly remember times when I was on stage playing with the band and an incredibly complex combination of paradiddles, triplets, cymbal hits and syncopated bass drum beats would come together for me in a way that I never would have imagined possible for me to pull off with such perfection. When I tried to duplicate what I had just done, I couldn't get it exactly on the mark as I had the first time.

For me this moment in time was almost like an epiphany, but I had heard other drummers who had practiced their craft with more diligence than I and this type of complex combination of beats was something that they could put together at any given moment and be confident that they would be "right on" every time. The reason it flowed all the time for them and could only happen for me at random moments was that they had trained their physical body to cooperate in unity with a series of their thoughts.

A drum teacher once told me, "Larry, if you can play a beat on the table with your fingers, then you can also play it on the drums. You just need to stop struggling with your drumsticks, bass pedal and high hat and simply let your body respond freely to the beats racing through your mind."

Being "on" in life does not have to be a random occurrence. It can become our predictable, everyday, normal operating procedure.

Well, while we have all had these "on" moments, we also know what it is like during the times when we are out of balance and we feel "off." It's like we are walking around with one shoe on and one shoe off.

We also know the contrast between being in the *flow* and the *struggle*. When we are trying to *get things* or trying to *get* other people's attention, we exude a sense of neediness.

When you feel that way and other people can sense that you are needy, your fragile emotional state makes it very easy for them to manipulate you in order for them to *get* what they want. Neediness also causes a built-in insecurity and feeling of lack. It is based on a philosophy and a belief that there is really not enough to go around, so you better *get* some, even if you have to settle for less than what would fulfill you.

Some people's philosophy is to "get all you can, can all you get, and sit on the can!" When you are *attracting*, you are receiving what you know already has your name on it. You're not taking it from someone else, and you're not receiving it by chance or by trickery. It was yours, waiting for you all along, and nobody has the right to take it away from you. Whenever it leaves your life, you know it means something better is supposed to take its place.

We also know the difference between *acting* and *reacting*. *Acting* is a point of strength; *reacting* throws you off balance and results in weakness.

The difference between *being* or just *doing* is the difference between the dog wagging the tail and the tail wagging the dog. If you are first *being* the Real You, then the everyday *doing* of life will have meaning and purpose and you will *be* inspired to *do* the things that take you closer to your dream-purpose.

Most people believe that to *be* someone great you have to *do* a lot of great things. This kind of thinking is backwards. *Being* who you really are is supposed to come first. That's when you become absolutely unstoppable and you know that you know that you know that your dream has your name on it.

Then you will not settle for less and you will not be denied. It will happen because it has to happen. No matter what your present circumstances look like, you can still know that you were born for freedom and that, as you make freedom principles your predominant way of thinking, it is just a matter of time before it will become your everyday life experience.

Where Your True Passion Is, There Will Your Treasure Be Also

We know what it is to really want something or someone so much that we would do just about anything to have what we want. Even a greater momentum is created when we know that what we are going after is supposed to be ours to help us *be* who we were meant to *be*.

We are all familiar with the feeling of being driven to have something or someone. If we really know that we want that house, car, boat, computer, piece of clothing or any other thing, then we will figure out a way to get it. Many times people will unwisely even get themselves into debt that exceeds their income because they act on impulse to receive this type of immediate gratification.

Likewise, when you fall in love with someone, almost immediately you know that you know that your number-one priority in life is to be with him or her even before going out on the first date.

I remember with crystal clarity the night that I met my wife, Julie. A friend of mine named Toby had invited me to go out on his boat to watch a meteor shower that was supposed to take place on a Sunday night. It promised to be a spectacular event, and it was reported on the news that hundreds of meteors would be flying through the heavens in clear view.

I arrived at the boat just after the sun had set. It was beginning to get dark; and, although I arrived right at the prearranged time, a few people had arrived before me. Toby informed us that we would set sail in just a few minutes, after a few more expected guests had arrived. I helped make a few adjustments to the sails of the boat, following the expert directions of Captain Toby, and then I sat down to relax and just gaze up at the heavens.

Just then Toby said, "Here they are!" I looked over at the dock and saw some people approaching but couldn't see their faces very clearly in the dark. Then Julie stepped onto the boat, and at that moment the rest of the world seemed to disappear.

"Wow!" I thought. "Who is that?" I immediately stood up and said, "Hi. I'm Larry," to which she gave me the expected response of "Hi. I'm Julie."

I looked directly at the ring finger on her left hand and was very relieved to see that there was no jewel there.

Well, I think I might have been doing a pretty good job of acting cool and collected on the outside, but on the inside I was jumping up and down. I was thinking, "I really hope she isn't already dating someone."

Well, fortunately she was not dating anyone at that time. I started talking with Julie, and after we had been cruising along for about twenty minutes I began to pick up the vibe that she might be thinking the same thoughts and feeling the same feelings about me that I was having about her. I won't fill you in on every minute of our voyage. But let's just say that as we watched in awe the hundreds of beautiful meteors blazing through the firmament, the meteor shower in the sky was a mild experience compared to the fireworks going off in our hearts.

While we were on the boat, Julie mentioned in the course of general conversation with everyone on board that she was probably going to need to move some furniture from the house she was living in. I was a little shy about asking her out on a date, but I did immediately offer to help move the furniture for her. At the end of the evening, I asked her for her phone number so that I could give her a call "to help her move her furniture."

To me, this "furniture move" became the number-one priority of the week. I thought, "This is great! I can help move the furniture and then ask her out on a date."

Well, it worked like a charm. I called Julie the next day and said, "I really think it would be a good idea if I stop by your place to see how much furniture you need to move so I will know what size truck to rent."

Now I realize that you know, Julie knew and I knew that I could have asked her to give me that information over the phone. But I guess it's pretty obvious that the whole furniture-moving thing was just an excuse to be able to see her again the day after we met without seeming overly anxious, and she was more than happy to play along.

Julie first allowed me to satisfy my strong desire to assess her furniture situation and then agreed to also go out to dinner with me the next night. I took her to eat at a nice restaurant near the water with a beautiful view of the lake. After dinner, we talked for several hours, though the time flew by so quickly that it seemed like a few minutes.

The next day I had to go to Washington, D.C., for a speaking engagement, and the number-one thing on my mind was being able to talk with Julie on the phone later that day. Before I left town, I stopped by a florist and ordered a dozen American Beauty long-stemmed red roses to be delivered to Julie with a card, on which I penned my most heartfelt thoughts.

Little did I know it, but Julie was thinking the same thing and was anxiously awaiting my phone call. By the time I called Julie from my hotel room in Washington, she had already received the roses and was ecstatic; and I must admit that I was beaming on the other end of the phone.

Isn't it amazing how everything else in life can all of a sudden move into second place when you fall in love? The world actually seems to be a different place than the one you were living in before you were struck with Cupid's arrow. You begin to put an unlimited amount of energy, creativity, strategy and sometimes even expense into winning the affections of the one on whom you are focused. You have a fire in your belly that cannot be put out. You are on a mission.

Well, a few years later, I took Julie back to the same restaurant down by the lake where we'd had our first date. This restaurant is also located about fifty yards from where the boat was docked on that first night when we met. I got on my knees in the middle of that restaurant, pulled a diamond ring out of my pocket and asked Julie if she would spend the rest of our lives together in marriage.

She said yes, we got married and today we are even happier to be together than we were that first week after we met. I am very thankful for such a wonderful, loving, supportive woman whom I have been blessed to be with. We inspire each other as we grow together with the purpose of keeping our love and commitment strong so that we never take for granted the gift of being together. Truly, the best part of our lives is still the time that Julie and I spend together.

You may have a similar story and may relate to the passion that two people can feel when they want to be together. Hollywood would not have been successful in making too many hit movies without this central theme of the lengths to which people will go when they are in love. It's never a question of "Will I be inconvenienced?" or "If it's not easy, then I will probably give up and quit." No way! Something all-consuming seems to take over. You will do and say things that under different circumstances would seem extreme, and you will even take the risk of looking like a fool while doing whatever it takes to be with that special someone.

The thoughts that you dwell on create your passions in life. Where your true passions are is also exactly where you will take immediate, consistent and relentless action.

Get out of the Way or Get Run Over— Mom Is on a Mission

My mother was an amazing Italian mom. She believed in me at a time when I didn't believe in myself, and I will be eternally grateful to her for her influence in my life. Like most Italian mothers of her generation, she felt that one of the most important tasks in life was cooking good food. She loved to cook and drew great satisfaction from caring for her family. I remember the hours that she spent in the kitchen each day. As I look back, I realize how much she enjoyed creating different dishes.

If you don't enjoy cooking, then it would probably be wise to take a different approach to food than the one she lived by. I also believe that we should eat to live and not live to eat. But if you know anything about the Italian culture, especially in the first, second and even third generations that came to America from Italy, eating and preparing savory dishes was right up there with the top two or three loves of life.

I remember an impressive happening that took place many times as a result of my mother's passion for food. At first it was puzzling to me, but after a while I grew to understand what caused my mother to move with such resolve and sense of purpose.

It would all start very early in the morning on any given day with my mother picking up the morning newspaper. All of a sudden, she would get this strange look in her eyes. It was kind of like "the eye of the tiger" in the Rocky movies when Sylvester Stallone, playing the role of Rocky Balboa, changes from being timid and insecure to the champion with fire in his eyes and an iron will to prevail even against seemingly insurmountable odds. Well, Mom would get this look in her eyes while reading that newspaper and immediately she would stand up and say, "Larry, put your coat on. We are going to Erie County Farms."

Erie County Farms is a market in my hometown where the surrounding farmers, as well as other suppliers, bring fresh produce, meats and other food items for sale. Each day the shelves, refrigerator cases, bushel baskets and crates in the aisles would be filled with fruits and vegetables that many times had just been picked from the field hours before. This market was also known for having the freshest meats at the lowest prices in the area.

What caused this fire to come into my mother's eyes with a totally focused sense of urgency to take immediate action? It was a small advertisement in the newspaper that read "Chickens 29 cents per pound." She would bundle me up even in the coldest of weather and quickly get me into the backseat of the car, and down the road we would go.

The first time I took this whirlwind trip to the market with my mother, I observed one of the most bewildering sights that I had ever beheld. She took my hand as we walked at a very fast pace (it was more like a controlled gallop), and she led me straight to a refrigerator case in the rear corner of the store. When we arrived there (as would also be the case each time this adventure would be repeated in the future), there was already a crowd of antsy men and women huddled around and pressed in as close to the refrigerator case as they could possibly get. My mom would find the best spot available and stand with one of her legs in front of the other. She would wedge her leading leg in between the two people in front of her to send a message to all those behind her that she was declaring this to be her territory.

Some of the women still had curlers in their hair. I could see that some of the men hadn't bothered to shave; some shirts were only half tucked in their trousers with the other half of the shirttails still hanging out. I remember that almost all the people there looked like they were in way too much of a hurry when they got dressed that morning, and they all had the same look in their eyes that my mother had in hers. It was a look that seemed to say, "There are some chickens here with my name on them, and I'm not leaving without them."

At first, I didn't know that there were even chickens involved in this scenario. All I could see were a bunch of "grown-ups" crowded tightly up against a refrigerated display case. Everything looks different to a child. For one thing, your eye level is different than adults'; you see the pieces of gum that have been stuck on the bottom of tables and counters and a lot of other things that adults miss out on. As a child, you view the world from a totally different camera angle.

But there are some advantages to being little; it's much easier to squeeze your way through a crowd when you're a whole lot shorter than most of the people there. I used my kid-powered curiosity to propel me into that crowd to see what all the fuss was about.

When I had finally pushed my way past all of those adult-sized kneecaps, I grabbed onto the top of the refrigerator case and pulled myself up high enough to look in. As I gazed in, I thought to myself, "What a waste that was to struggle through that forest of pants and dresses to see this!" My disappointment was fueled by the fact that the case was totally empty! Just seeing the bare walls and floor of the case was not much of a reward after all that effort.

Just as I was about to turn around and press my way back through the throng, I saw that there was more to this saga still unfolding before my eyes. Suddenly, a swinging door opened from the back room; I could see a little man with bent shoulders wearing a white apron speckled with blood.

Slowly, he began to wheel his cart towards the case. Every head in the crowd turned and followed the little man. With each step he took, the aggregate anticipation of his captive audience created an electric feeling in the air. Each person's neck adjusted with his every move as to not break the laser-beam glare fixed on this courier of each one's desire.

Finally, he arrived at the opposite side of the refrigerator case with only four feet between him and the anxious throng. He reached his hand toward his cart, which was overflowing with chickens in clear plastic bags, grabbed hold of one of them, then threw it into the empty cavity of the refrigerator case. Before it even hit the bottom of the case, an awaiting customer caught it in midair. This frontrow customer put the chicken in her shopping cart and turned around to get another one from the butcher's hand. When she turned to get her second chicken, a person behind her snatched the first chicken out of her shopping cart, put it in her own cart and looked in the other direction pretending nothing had happened.

I could hardly believe my eyes; I had just witnessed a chicken theft in progress. The crowd whipped into a frenzy of excitement; and my mom, determined to put ownership on three of those featherless critters for her family's upcoming dinners, was right in the middle of all the action. For all of that waiting and all of that energy, thought-power, strategy and persistence, what was the purpose? "Chickens 29 cents per pound!"

Now don't misunderstand me, I have stood in line for something that I really wanted to purchase; and if it was a really great deal, I have arrived early and stayed late to make sure that I secured whatever it was that I wanted to buy. But here's the point: if we will do that for a chicken, a suit of clothes, a car, a house or a sale of some kind, what about our dream-purpose? **Many people can get very focused on something that is temporary and will even rearrange their life to get something that will last for only a relatively short amount of time; but they are unable to maintain the same focus to go after their dream-purpose, which will last them a lifetime and allow them to leave a legacy for their loved ones, blessing yet unborn generations.**

You see, my mom did get three chickens that day! When she had positioned herself and marked off her territory in that crowd of competitors, I knew that, whatever it took, she would not leave that market empty-handed.

What does it take to keep that kind of focus, passion and determination on your dreams in life? For your dream-purpose to be fully manifested, it's obviously not going to be like a quick trip to the store. It will take a continual flow of passion and energy to hang in there even when things don't seem to be going as well or as quickly as you may have hoped.

How do you overcome discouragement and procrastination? How do you reach your own personal critical mass and see your breakthrough take place? How do you achieve freedom in every area of your life?

It's All About Freedom

It all starts with some type of daily approach to creating positive thought replacement. With this type of daily program, each day you are putting more principle-based thoughts on the right side of your scale.

At first it may not seem like much of a change is taking place, but very soon you will start to feel better about yourself and your life. When you have this shift in perspective, it causes an automatic positive change in your personal posture.

When your personal posture, or charisma, improves, this causes you to become the right kind of magnet and you start to attract the right people into your life. You start coming up with some really creative ideas. Then an opportunity is placed in front of you, or an opportunity that was there all along is suddenly revealed to be the next real step toward your dream.

But that beautiful new beginning or great next step would not have taken place if you hadn't placed that first positive-principle thought on the right side of your scale.

You simply continue to proceed by planting one thought at a time, until your breakthrough takes place and you are living your tangible dream-purpose.

Now, let's break this down to take a look at exactly how thoughts change us and then ultimately change our personal world. We have collected thoughts our entire life. We have received them from family, friends, education, television, radio, printed materials, society—and the list of sources goes on and on and on.

The total collection of the *thoughts* we have accepted creates our *philosophy*. Our *philosophy* creates our *reality*, and our *reality* will cause us to create our *life experience*. Our outer life matches our particular inner perception of the different areas of our life as well as our reality about our life as a whole.

If you sum up in one word the final outcome and result of the process of "renewing your mind," the final and permanent life experience that occurs is freedom. Spiritual freedom, mental freedom, emotional freedom, physical freedom, financial freedom and relational freedom become more and more of your living reality every day.

It is possible for a person to appear free in one or several areas of life but still be living under an overall heavy sense of restriction. For example, there are those who seem free spiritually but whose finances are a mess. Others seem to be financially secure but are living with great restrictions spiritually, mentally and emotionally. Still others have everything seemingly flowing in their life, except in their relationships with other people.

As we look closely at these contrasts, we can easily see how all of these areas of life are most definitely connected to each other. Therefore, a lack of freedom in one area of life can most definitely lower your level of freedom even in the other areas that you are stronger in. For true, freedom-producing critical mass to take place, we must be open to having our mind renewed in every area of our life. The 87 percent negative self-talk that most people labor under results in an overall 87 percent restriction in their life.

We can easily evaluate what areas of our life contain the larger percentages of our negative self-talk. All you have to do is take an honest look at the different areas of your life. The areas in which you are experiencing the highest levels of love, faith, peace, security and freedom are the same areas in which you have a great number of true, principle-based thoughts and a small amount of negative, falsity-based self-talk. In the areas that you are experiencing the highest levels of fear, doubt, stress, insecurity and restriction, you have a high level of negative, falsity-based self-talk and a small number of true, principle-based thoughts.

Truly effective thought replacement and critical mass can only take place in your thought life when you are working on renewing your mind in every area of your life. Now in the last paragraph I said, "All you have to do is take an honest look at the different areas of your life." By saying "all you have to do," I am by no means implying that this is a casual process. You literally have to come clean with yourself about your fears, doubts, insecurities and restrictions. Until you identify the areas of your life that need the most work, you cannot begin a focused approach with your personal program of thought replacement.

It is important to understand that taking personal inventory and coming clean about the areas of your life in which you are living in fear, insecurity, doubt and restriction is not a matter of getting obsessed with your weaknesses. The key to ridding yourself of these hindrances is not to thoroughly dissect each problem but to simply discover and acknowledge the areas of your life that need to be changed and then go to work on them.

Working on removing fear from your life is not accomplished by finding the fear and trying to dig it up by the roots as if it were a weed growing in your flowerbed. It is obvious that people do not enjoy having fears and insecurities and would like to get rid of them. But we need to stay continually cognizant of the fact that the fear or insecurity is only a symptom of a deficiency of truth-based reality in an individual's life.

To remove the symptoms of weakness, the cause must be eliminated. It is not focusing on the problem that sets us free. It is a matter of shifting our concentration to a steady diet of true, principle-based thoughts.

The more centered we become on what is true in our spirit, in relationships, in prosperity, in our purpose and in every other area of our life, the freer we become spiritually, mentally, emotional, physically and financially. This is the process that results in our being free to focus our energy to do all of the things that are necessary to manifest our tangible dream-purpose in our inner and outer life.

Therefore, the only productive reason for finding the problem areas of our life is to know where we need to concentrate the most on receiving an infusion of true, principle-based reality thoughts. This will give us an indication of what books we need to read, what tapes we need to listen to, what people we need to spend more or less time with and so forth.

A deliberate, targeted strategy is needed to ensure that you are receiving the new thoughts that will cause you to conceive and give birth to the dream-purpose you were born to live. I will give you some suggestions later on in this book. A major part of this targeted strategy includes a daily program for your life that will give you a track to run on in the pursuit of renewing your mind. But for right now, let's first take a look at how to simply and accurately assess the different areas of your life.

Honest Self-Assessment

At this point, I am going to give you an exercise that you can do in about five minutes. I encourage you to do this exercise as quickly as possible. Most of the areas of life in which we settle for less than what is rightfully ours are areas we have rationalized to the point that we have begun to believe we are experiencing all that is possible for us. "Overthinking" with the "natural, common mind" always leads to the formulation of a series of thoughts that justify our lack of total freedom in life. This overthinking is reinforced by the negative self-talk that already dominates our mind.

If we are frustrated or restricted in an area of life, or in our life as a whole, it is because of the wrong thoughts we have already collected. Therefore, performing this exercise by running an assessment through the same "mental computer program" already filled with errors will only lead to further rationalization.

You can only know what is "truly real" in the Real You, which is the purposeful, love-filled, honest You. So do this exercise from your gut reaction, not overthinking, but writing down the first response that comes from your heart.

I perform this assessment on myself either once per week or, at the very least, once per month; and I am often surprised with what I come up with. I often find blind spots in my life that I did not realize existed. Therefore, I am able to deal with them while they are small rather than allowing a fear or restriction to grow for months or even years.

This is a simplified version of an exercise that I have used and taught in the past. When we are dealing with things of the heart, it is best to keep it as simple as possible to avoid accessing the old ways of thinking that have kept us on a lower level to begin with. One way that our outer self attempts to avoid change is to overcomplicate what is very simple so that further procrastination can be justified. So let's keep it real and to-the-point.

Sit down with a piece of paper, and on the left-hand side list the different areas of your life. They include but are not limited to your spirit, mind, emotions, finances, relationships and career. Other areas may be your lifestyle, your spouse or the person you are dating or in an exclusive love relationship with, your children, your physical body and your dream-purpose. Just take a few minutes to list all of the areas of your life that you can think of. Don't worry about leaving an area of your life out. You can always add more areas to your list the next time you do this exercise.

Now after you have completed your list, go back up to the top of the list and read the first area of your life that you wrote down. As you read the individual word that signifies each particular area of your life, say these two words to yourself in the form of a question: "freedom or restriction?" One of these words will come up stronger from your heart than the other; again, I encourage you to not give in to the temptation to overthink or begin to justify your answer in any way. *What it is, is what it is; and the way it is, is exactly the way it is;* and realizing this is the first step to making it different than the way it is at this moment.

Immediately after you have read that specific area of your life and asked yourself the question "freedom or restriction?" on the right-hand side of the paper, quickly write down either the word "freedom" or the word "restriction." After you have completed the first area of your life, quickly move on to the second area, then the third and so forth.

When you have responded in this exercise to all of the areas of your life written in the left-hand column, then go back up to the top of the list again and look at what you wrote in the right-hand column. Any area of your life that has the word "freedom" next to it is an area in which you have collected a great number of true, principle-based thoughts throughout your life. Any area of life that has the word "restriction" next to it is an area of life in which you have collected a great number of false, error-based thoughts.

How can we be sure that this is an effective approach to assessing and centering our life? It is very simple: "when you KNOW the truth, it makes you free." If we are not free in any specific area of our life, it just means that we need to come to know some new thoughts to begin the freedom process.

Moving Beyond Restrictions

As you are taking a look at your list, simply acknowledge that any area of your life that has the word "restriction" next to it is an area that you need to work on to create critical mass. Critical mass is accomplished by bombarding that area of your thought life with the right thoughts.

Read books. Listen to inspirational and educational teaching tapes or CDs that feed you the right thoughts in these specific areas. Prayer and meditation are wonderful influences for renewing your mind. Make sure you find a way to spend as much time as possible in the presence of quality people who are strong in the areas that you are weak in.

As you keep thought replacement at the top of your priority list, day by day you will get closer and closer to your own personal critical mass in specific areas and also in your life as a whole. Keep going, even if it doesn't seem to be making much of a difference during the first few days. In fact, as you begin to renew your mind, the first thing that you may experience is a feeling of resistance from your old way of thinking. Keep the momentum up, and your old thought patterns will begin to loose their grip; and, on the inside, you will have an absolute knowing that will replace the doubts, fears and insecurities that once hindered you. Also, you will see a chain reaction of manifested outward benefits that result from the thought-based critical mass and chain reaction that has occurred on the inside. The process for true success in any endeavor always follows the pattern of an inner change that results in an outward expression.

You will meet the right people and discover the right opportunities, or all of a sudden your eyes will be opened to the opportunities that were right in front of you all along. You will naturally begin to *attract* love, great relationships, spiritual blessings, finances, peace and many other benefits, instead of trying to force things to happen. You will begin to *be* and not just *do*, *flow* and not *struggle*, *act* in life and not *react* to circumstances and people.

Our dream-life is not something we can force into existence. We must know that it already belongs to us and then take the steps necessary to make it happen. Yes, we have to *do* all of the outer activity, and often it takes willingness on our part to maintain a stronger work ethic than the average person's to bring our dream-purpose into manifestation. But for it to be real, lasting and fulfilling, all of our *doing* must become a natural outgrowth and byproduct of the freedom process that enables us to "shake off" the weights that would hold us back and truly be purely who we really are.

Now I realize that we live in a world that seems to be obsessed with outward appearances and that you may feel you are in the minority operating with a much lower amount of negative self-talk than the average person. But you are in good company because all of the other people on the planet who are truly living a free life are also in the minority.

Common thinking causes people to become completely absorbed with trying to fix their inner needs from the outside, and this leads to discouragement, frustration and defeatism. Remember, your physical body, mind, will and emotions were given to you as tools to use in building and manifesting your dream-purpose. But the creator, the writer, the inspirer, the dreamer, the resilient one, the persistent person, the one who will not settle for less than the highest level that he or she was born to live on is *who you are* on the inside. The outward evidence of your dream is simply proof that you have been using the tools you have been given with inspiration and strategy in alignment with the destiny available to you all along in the Real You.

Again, we all know what it is like to experience temporary motivation, which evaporates over a period of minutes, hours or even days. The reason for this lack of ability to hold on to motivation is revealed in the very nature of motivation itself. Motivation is not self-powered and by itself has a very short "shelf life" or "life span." Motivation is something that we experience in the "outer self" (mind, will, emotions and physical body).

Simply stated, if you stay inspired by your dream-purpose on the inside, then motivation will be automatic and continuous in your outward life. Your level of ability to stay inspired on the inside depends on the quality of your thoughts. Isn't it interesting how just about everything comes back to what's happening in your thought life? *As a man or woman thinketh, so shall they be and so it will show up in their everyday outer life experience.*

Most people do not set out to live a life in which they feel like a failure or live in restriction, frustration and lack. It is not usually a person's deliberately planned-out strategy to live a life of doom. Failure, sadness and dissatisfaction fill our lives a little bit every day, just as do success, happiness and fulfillment. One of the greatest dangers is that through our daily activity routine and "doing" of life we will miss our critical mass and never be able to live a total life of freedom. It is also true that the freedom to live and enjoy the blessings that you showed up on this planet to experience comes by continuing to add a little bit to the right side of the scale on a day-by-day, minute-by-minute and second-by-second basis.

It's in Your Hands

Years ago, I heard a man tell a story about something called the Touch Stone. This story is about a man who heard about a stone that had a very special and miraculous quality. It was said that whoever held this stone in hand would be able to wish for anything and be granted that wish. This amazing piece of rock was called the Touch Stone because the first person to touch it would receive its amazing benefit.

Becoming thoroughly convinced that this story was true, the man sold all of his possessions and set out on a journey to find this unique piece of rock. The Touch Stone was black in color, and this presented a problem because during his quest to find the stone he found that its location obscured its visibility. The exact geographical spot that his search would need to be carried out was on the banks of the Black Sea. It would be very difficult to comb an average coastline, examining each black stone until he found the object of his desire. But the Black Sea presented a heightened challenge because the banks of this particular body of water were made up of nothing but black sand and black stones.

Wow! What an undertaking this would be! But he set out with total resolve that whatever the personal cost or investment of time required, it would all be worth it when he held this precious item in his hands.

Other than its color, there was one more way to distinguish the Touch Stone from the billions of other pieces of rock on the planet. This peculiarity also was signified in its name. The Touch Stone was always warm. It had some sort of inner heat source that kept it independently warm to the touch, even when everything around it was at a cooler temperature.

The man set out on his long trip and finally arrived at the edge of the Black Sea. As he gazed up and down the coastline, he must have been overcome with the enormity of the seemingly insurmountable task that lay before him. But he certainly hadn't come all this way to give up.

He knew that he would have to use some type of systematic approach to sort through the entire beach to find this one stone that was no bigger than the palm of his hand. So he decided to begin his expedition at one end of the coastline, working his way up and down the beach, carefully examining a little section at a time, then moving on, knowing that all of the area behind him had been eliminated.

Since the only way to distinguish the Touch Stone from the other stones on the beach was to see if it had this independently warm quality, he could not effectively conduct his search during the daytime hours. The intense sun beating down on the beach would make all of the stones hot to the touch. Therefore, he would wait until the sun went down each evening and all of the other stones on the shoreline were cold, then search all night until the sun came up the next morning.

Soon he discovered that he became confused as to which stones he had picked up to evaluate and which ones he had not yet handled. So he added one more step to his process of elimination. Once he picked up a stone to see whether it was warm or cold, he began throwing every cold stone into the water so that the only stones left on the beach were sure to be those that he had not yet touched. His system seemed foolproof.

Night after night turned into week after week and then month after month, but he was determined to make his dream a reality. Just about all of his waking hours each night were dominated with this one activity. He would pick up a stone, find it to be cold and throw it into the water; then pick up another, find it to be cold and throw it into the water. A ten-hour shift with an average of a thirty-second examination of each stone would add up to 1200 stones per night.

The repetition became quite monotonous, but he knew that once he found the Touch Stone his life would be marvelous from that moment on. As he held this vision, he would continue to press forward picking up cold stones and throwing them in the water, picking up more stones and throwing them in the water. Then one night, having repeated this ritual hundreds of times in the previous hours, he picked up a stone and threw it—and just as it left his hand, he realized that it had been warm!

It is not always the big challenges of life that stop a person from living one's dream-purpose and enjoying all of the benefits that go along with it. **In fact, many times the instances in our lives when we seem to be facing insurmountable odds are the very points on the path of life that we can look back to and realize were a "blessing in disguise."** The roadblock that we had to overcome literally served as a catalyst for our higher good.

The smaller, everyday habits and patterns of our daily life are far subtler and over time serve as a much greater threat. The days, weeks, months, years and even decades can fly by, and when we look back it can seem as if we have been spinning our wheels. Life can become nothing more than a series of days in which we wake up every morning simply to "get stuff done," then fall wearily into bed each night only to wake up the next morning to repeat the same pattern all over again.

Life was never meant to be a struggle. Life is meant to be something more than just chasing a carrot that one never seems to catch. It is sad to say, but a lot of people on their deathbeds look back on their lives and realize that they spent most of their time making a living but never really lived. They worked a number of jobs, bought a lot of groceries, financed cars and houses, enjoyed some social activities, ate a lot of food, paid their bills and taxes, and in their spare time watched television and rented hundreds or possibly thousands of videos. Even the fact that they had the joy of rearing some beautiful children is often tainted with the conscious or subconscious awareness that they never gave their children one of the most important gifts. They were busy putting clothes on their backs and food in their stomachs. They were teaching them to be good people and making sure that they were provided for with the finest education possible; but they never gave their children a living example of a parent who is living his or her dream-purpose. Unless these children are fortunate enough to find a mentor who will guide them to greatness, they will often follow the same treadmill existence that their parents demonstrated to them.

But this prison sentence of boredom does not have to be served through inheritance. This cycle of purposelessness can be interrupted by any individual who makes a quality decision to break the generational chain by becoming transformed by the renewing of one's mind.

Seize This Day

Your purpose is your Touch Stone. I believe that the very fact that you are still reading this book is evidence that you have decided to not let life pass you by. It is always "today," in the present tense. At 12:00 A.M., yesterday became today; and tonight at exactly sixty seconds after 11:59 P.M., tomorrow will become today. Someone once said, "Yesterday is a cancelled check, tomorrow is a promissory note, but only today is usable currency."

Someone may say, "I feel like I have already thrown my stone into the water. I saw my opportunity come and go, but I missed it." Well, it's not over until it is over. Some of the greatest success stories of all time are of people who have gone bankrupt five or ten times or were told that they would never make it, but they decided to get up one more time and press forward. The important thing is not how many times you fall down. The important thing is whether you keep on getting back up.

It is not impossible to dive into the water with some scuba gear and find our "purpose stone" again. In fact, there are several times in most of our lives that we go off course and have to get back "on purpose" again.

Thought replacement on a daily, continual basis is the only surefire, guaranteed way to avoid getting stuck on the same treadmill that is most common-thinking people's life experience. Now when I say "common-thinking people," I am in no way implying that anyone is any better than anyone else. Every person is just as precious and just as important as every other individual. There are no "big shots" and no "little shots." There are also no big purposes and no little purposes; there are only REAL PURPOSES. The person who breaks away from the pack and lives on a daily purpose-powered quest of having one's mind continually renewed is not any better than a common-thinking person, but such a person *will* ultimately end up much better off.

Beginning with the next chapter, we are going to look at the ingredients that make up our thought-replacement, mind-renewing program. This program is more than just something to use when we are feeling down. It is a lifestyle that is interwoven into the fabric of each day to help us avoid being down in the first place. If we are going to think differently and therefore change our philosophy, our reality and our life experience, then it is crystal clear that we will have to find some different thought-food sources than those that the average common-thinking person feeds on. Before the conclusion of this book, we will work with many of the other facets and components of how to live on higher and higher levels of thought replacement.

In the following chapter, we will look at a major impacting influence on our thoughts and perceptions in life, as well as a source that enables us to have a greater vision for the future. This next, vital ingredient is one that you will find without exception in the life of every person who has lived, or is living, one's dream-purpose. Now, let's move on to the next chapter together and see the amazing possibilities that *being mentored* and *being a mentor* hold for us in the treasure chest of life.

Chapter 5

The Mentor Principle

Many people walk in and out of your life,
But only true friends will leave their footprints in your heart...
Learn from the mistakes of others;
You can't live long enough to make them all your self...
Friends, you and me...you brought a friend...
And now there are three...we started a group...
Our circle of friends...and like that circle...
There is no end...
Yesterday is history.
Tomorrow is mystery.
Today is a gift.

—ELEANOR ROOSEVELT

Some people look in the mirror to see who they are—but if you really want to know who you are, look at the friends that you choose.

—CHINESE PROVERB

Among all of the successful and heroic figures of modern days and throughout history, you will seldom find one individual who has accomplished great things without having a mentor and being a mentor to others.

In the previous chapters, we examined the effect that our thoughts have on our lives. Very few influences have as strong of an effect on how we think than the one that we are going to deal with in this chapter. The people whom we look to as examples in life and whom we choose to spend our quality time with are a major part of the impacting process that results in what we embrace as true or false thoughts.

There is a saying that "birds of a feather flock together." This is a very accurate statement. If you are not like the other "birds" when you first join the group, over time you will become like them in thought and deed. Those whom we open ourselves up to can influence us toward any one of the following: (1) greater and higher levels to reach for, (2) a level to become stagnant on or (3) a lower level to fall down to.

If we are to go higher in life and realize our dream-purpose, we will not make the journey alone. There is the occasional example of a person who has had tremendous breakthroughs in life while locked up in solitary confinement or concentration camp or trapped on a desert island. But even when you read or hear those people's stories, you will find that in their forced solitude they drew on the past example of a person who had a positive influence on them.

The *"mentor principle"* is very clearly seen in apprenticeship programs. For example, a master carpenter will take a novice under his wing and teach his student the trade. In some professional and specialty areas, such as medicine, you are not even permitted to perform what you learn during your many years of formal education until you spend a predetermined number of hours working under the watchful eye of a seasoned professional.

How is it that most people see this principle of *"being mentored and being a mentor"* as absolutely necessary and even mandatory in certain pursuits but don't realize that going after their dreams in life will usually require learning from someone who has proven to be successful in pursuing and living one's dream.

From a mentor you learn skills and talents, as well as hard cold facts, systems and strategies that you can follow to reach the desired results in any endeavor. The natural skills that you learn from a dream-purpose mentor, though they are important, are only part of the equation. **Some things are better "caught" than "taught." For example, there are many people who never considered that they could live their life on a higher, more prosperous level until they got a taste of what that higher level looked like and felt like while hanging around their mentor.** They may have been perfectly willing to accept the destiny of living a life of boredom until they had a good dose of seeing a person who gets up each day with a passion to make a real, positive difference in one's own life and in the lives of others. An individual can see financial struggles and lack as just an unavoidable part of life until that person meets and really gets to know someone who is financially independent. Getting a taste for a better, and even the best, spiritual, mental, emotional, physical, financial and relational life possible by observing others enjoying it is a big part of becoming open to a larger vision for your own life.

Removing Inherited Limiting Perceptions

Once you see "close up" how it was possible for someone else to live one's dream-purpose, you will begin to realize that it's possible for you too.

One of the greatest advantages of having a mentor is to be able to get a whole new perspective of the possibilities that we have missed or were not exposed to in our childhood and teenage years. Depending on your particular childhood experiences, you may feel that the mentoring that your parents gave you would fall into one of these categories: great, good, fair, bad or maybe, in some cases, even abusive. But many of us can probably point back to areas where we feel that our parents did a great job of mentoring us. Conversely, though they may have even been doing the best they knew how, there could be some areas in which we know their mentoring had a negative effect on our thought processes.

I was influenced while growing up in my particular family to see financial restriction as a way of life. My dad worked several jobs throughout his life, but it always seemed that he could only find employment as a physical laborer working under some of the harshest conditions. But regardless of the hardships he had to endure, I don't ever remember my father complaining; and he was always faithful to put food on the table, clothing on our backs and a roof over our heads. He is a dear, wonderful man. You will not find a gentler or more giving man on earth.

My dad, who is now eighty-one years old, served in the army and then worked for the Pennsylvania Railroad for a number of years fixing locomotives, mostly in the outdoors. In those days, the winter weather was much more severe in Pennsylvania than it is today. The winters were long with below-zero temperatures and three to six feet of snow being very common. The summers were just the opposite, with the humidity very high and very hot. So he would come home each night exhausted from the hard physical labor coupled with the inclement weather.

Then, one day, he got a layoff notice and had to look for another job. After months of searching, he was becoming very discouraged. Finally, he had to start receiving assistance from the government, and our diet consisted of mostly surplus food.

Surplus food was food that was provided by the government to those in need, and the variety of edible choices would make a hot dog look like a gourmet meal. There was canned beef, canned potatoes and canned pork. Well, you get the idea: our menu mainly consisted of pretty much anything that they could put in a can. There was also a variety of three different surplus cheeses, along with several other staple items.

My mom did the best she could; but, with those surplus ingredients, even the most creative cook couldn't make a meal that would even come close to passing a taste test. Basically, no matter how you fixed this stuff, it always ended up tasting more like the can it came in than the food it was supposed to resemble.

Well, Dad was out of work for a number of years, and life was very challenging. There was always real love in our home, but the financial pressures and lack always seemed to put a damper on things. Either the house payment could not be made that month, or the car broke down and there wasn't enough money to fix it—along with a host of other limitations that caused a constant atmosphere of insecurity about the future.

Finally, my father landed a job working on boilers for steam-powered systems. Again, the work was physically abusive with lots of kneeling on concrete and exposure to toxic fumes as well as other harsh elements. No matter how hard my dad worked, and even when he took a second job and my mom started working outside the home at a butcher shop, it still didn't seem that he and my mother could make ends meet financially.

Dad was fifty-seven when my mom died. For a few years he lived independently and his health was good. But once his physical problems began, his health slowly declined over the years. This was quite a change because as I was growing up, I don't remember my dad being sick a single day. Then he had a series of small strokes that took quite a toll on him. After his first stroke, I moved him in to live with me.

For seven years, my dad lived with me. Finally, his health got to the point that, with my busy traveling schedule, I began to realize he could no longer get along without me there. I hired a nurse to come and be with him on a daily basis and continued to increase the number of hours that she would spend with him, until finally it became clear that it was no longer going to meet his needs to live with me. I would come home after being out of town and find him having some real physical challenges that indicated that he needed continuous care in a medical environment. So I found a nice place for him to live with an excellent nursing staff.

When I'm on the road, I will call him from the hotel or an airport and tell him that I'll be home the next day and will come to pick him up and take him out to eat some of his favorite food at an Italian restaurant. For the first thirty seconds of each phone call, he can't speak to me because he is too choked up with fighting back the tears. I can always hear him on the other end of the line trying to regain his composure. Finally, he'll get a few words out and say, "Okay, Larry, I'll see you tomorrow," and then he'll start getting choked up again and have difficulty speaking.

When I get back in town and go to pick him up, he will often be sitting in a chair in the front lobby. A nurse or security guard will frequently inform me that he has been sitting there waiting for hours, even though they would try to tell him that I would not be arriving for quite sometime. He will often even refuse to leave his watch-post to eat because he is sure that they are mistaken and that I will be walking through that door any minute. When I arrive at the time that I have promised and he sees me walk through the door, again, he will fight back the tears and my heart is always greatly moved as I give him a hug and a kiss and tell him that I love him.

His example of a loyal, loving, faithful and giving spirit always greatly impacted my life and still does to this day. He always stood by me as I was pursuing my dreams, and you'd better not say anything bad to him about his boy or you will get a strong and emphatic rebuke! I thank God for giving me such a wonderful dad who did his best mentoring me in the key areas of his strengths and character.

I talked about my mother a lot in my last book and will add here that she also was wonderful in so many ways. She held the vision for me for seventeen years, telling me constantly that I was born to travel the world helping people. The exact words that she repeated to me thousands of times were "Larry, you're going to grow up, have a message burning on your heart and speak to crowds of tens of thousands of people." How she knew that to be a fact is a story that I will not repeat here because I already talked about it in detail in my last, previously mentioned book.* But let's just say that she knew that she knew that she knew this to be my destiny.

For seventeen years, I looked, acted, smelled, walked and talked in a way that was just the opposite of anybody that ten people would want to listen to. I continually disappointed my parents and put them through unmitigated hell on earth, but my mom still continued to hold that vision in front of me. The beautiful thing about this is that my mom did live long enough to see the fruits of her labor. In fact, just thirty days before my mother died I gave my first talk to a group of people. My mom sat right in the front row and watched her boy begin the journey she held a vision of reality for through so many trying years.

The last days of my mother's life were very precious to both of us. They were filled with a depth of love and honesty that I will always remember and cherish. I was blessed to be there to hold her in my arms as she spoke her last words and took her last breath. Well, needless to say, I am very thankful for my parents.

Unlearning and Relearning

No matter how wonderful your home life was and how many positive thoughts you may have received from teaching or by example, there are probably a few things that you needed to unlearn and relearn after you were no longer

---

*The Resilient Power of Purpose, formerly titled How To Be Purpose Driven.

living under your parent's roof. Maybe your childhood home life was a very bad example and you learned how you did not want to live. Whether your home life was good or bad, there are always areas in which you are going to need to learn from new mentors who have something to impart to you that the mentoring of your parents could not supply.

Don't Miss It

Though I will be eternally grateful for being raised in a home where I learned so many of the most important things that money cannot buy, I also learned the reality of how financial struggles and worries can create an atmosphere of gloom and put negativity in the very air that fills the house. It wasn't a matter of mismanaging money; my mother was a very meticulous steward of the dollars that were there. The problem was that there were never enough dollars to cover the bare necessities of life, let alone an "extra cushion" or the resources to take a vacation or enjoy the wonderful, abundant world that lay beyond our doorstep. I knew in my heart that this kind of financial bondage was not what we were born to endure. So, early on in life, I began to study the lives of people who were prospering—not only in financial freedom, but also in all of the other areas of their lives.

Shortly after getting out of high school, I had the good fortune of meeting a man who ran a successful construction business and had a wonderful family. His mentoring was like an introductory course that prepared me for other mentors and teachers who would come along later in my life. I learned from his example that **the possibilities for our lives are as large or as small as we presently believe them to be.** It was a great time of preparing the soil of my mind for the seeds that would be planted later, but I was still too much of a novice to grasp many of the principles that I was seeing him live by and practice on a daily basis.

Then, a few years later, I met another gentleman who really broadened my vision for prosperity and also gave me an example of what it really was like to love life and live every day to its fullest. I could see that financially he was living in a totally different place than I had ever seen "close up." He made more money in one week than I was making in an entire year, and he gave money away to causes that he believed in and had plenty to spare. This abundance enabled him and his family to enjoy a lifestyle of a higher quality than I had ever witnessed firsthand. Of course, I had seen this type of freedom-lifestyle portrayed in a movie or on TV, but seeing it "up close and personal" sparked a belief in my heart that it could be possible for me too.

I spent several years working very closely with this gentleman but was still not ready to see beneath the surface of the outer blessings that he and his family were enjoying. I thought I was getting the secrets of life and the principles for happiness and success. But after concluding my years of work with him, when I tried to duplicate the success that I had viewed firsthand in his life, I concluded that I must have missed some of the main points I should have been concentrating on. I realized that, even though the answers, the principles and the pattern were right in front of me, somehow I had "missed it."

It is a terrible feeling to know that you had a chance and missed it, and it is an even worse feeling to wonder when or if you will get another chance. So, for the next nine years, I continued to live with the same limited thinking, financial struggles and atmosphere of gloom that I had watched my parents deal with while I was growing up.

A Third Chance

I began to wonder if maybe I had blown the last opportunity that I would have to learn to be free through the coaching of a real, live example. I was ready to do whatever it would take to be able to have another chance to learn the lessons I had missed the first and second times around. It was at this point—when I had become 100 percent open, hungry and ready to learn—that I met another great man whom I believed to be qualified to be my next mentor.

I went to great lengths to get in the presence of this potential life coach because I certainly didn't want to spend another nine years wandering around in the wilderness of ignorance. I needed help to get to my next higher level, and I needed it *now!*

Several qualities struck me very strongly about this man. These were similar areas of wisdom and strength that were also evident in the previous mentor from whom I had been privileged to receive tutelage. He loved his family, he had a great passion for life and he was resolute about being totally purpose-driven in everything that he did or said. Another reason that I valued the opportunity to be coached by him was that he had a flow of prosperity in his life that was also very similar to my last mentor's. In fact, he had tapped even more into the principles of prosperity, to the extent that he made more money in one hour than I was making while working an entire month of forty- to fifty-hour workweeks.

It is amazing how we all have the same twenty-four hours in a day, but the prosperity that one person attracts in the same day, week, month or year can be so drastically different from what another person with the same outward advantages attracts.

Of course, if you don't have love, peace, fulfillment, purpose, great relationships and a balanced life, all the money in the world won't bring you joy or happiness. But one fact that cannot be denied is that few things will rob a person of more joy, cause more stress, anxiety, ulcers and interfamily discord than perpetual financial worries. I like what I have heard quoted many times: "Money may not be important, but it's right up there with oxygen." If you don't believe it, just try living without any money for a few months!

So when I had an opportunity to be mentored by this third gentleman who could teach me the same lessons that I had missed the first and second times around, I dove in headfirst to learn all I could; and I was absolutely determined and focused on not missing anything.

This *"mentor principle"* is very simple. What needs to happen for this principle to work for you, for you to benefit from a mentor, is that you find someone to whom you can relate and whom you respect with confidence that he or she is operating on the higher level that you want to reach. Then you find a way to be able to be in this person's presence on a consistent basis. Most of the time, this will involve your serving the person in some capacity that will be a blessing to him or her personally in a cause or purpose that the person is involved in, in the person's business or family.

Well, this time I made a deliberate effort to look beneath the surface to observe the cause and effect of the treasure of thoughts and actions this mentor was demonstrating. I took good notes and learned from this mentor's words and example the basics of prosperity principles, as well as the importance of a strong work ethic.

Over time, I found myself duplicating the level of

success that he was on when I first met him, and now I have even exceeded that level to go still higher. Of course, the same principles and strategies that he taught and that I caught from him have continued to work in his personal and professional life with results that have caused him to head for the stars and beyond!

The Inside Track

Another way that your mentor can help you is to not only show you the best way to operate according to true principles but also to give you the "inside scoop" on what "not to do." I have heard people say that "experience is the best teacher." While I do not disagree that at times your own personal happenings in life can serve as a catalyst for positive change, there are many cases in which you will find that "other people's experiences" can be an even better teacher.

You have probably had this experience of people giving you driving directions to get to a specific location: they will tell you that the best way to get your destination is to take a route that actually seems like "the long way around." But because they know the area so well, they can warn you that on the shorter route there is a bridge out, or you will be traveling on mainly bumpy dirt roads, or there is some other reason why the way that looks the best on the map is not necessarily the most advantageous route to take. The only reason they have that valuable information to share with you is that they have been there.

Why run into brick walls that someone else has already slammed into and can tip you off about so that you can avoid the time and frustration of having to regroup and get back on track? **A mentor can show you where the landmines are planted and also where the gold is buried.**

Once I witnessed, through watching the example of a mentor, what it was like to live a life of freedom, I began to believe that I could realize the same kind of blessings. Then my belief continued to grow until it produced a strong sense of worthiness.

Knowing that you are worthy of freedom in every area of your life is vital in order to make your dream-purpose a reality. If you do not feel worthy of living a blessed life, then one of two things will happen: (1) you will never get to your next higher level, or (2) even if you do work your way to your next higher level of freedom, you will sabotage yourself to make sure that you'll drop back down to the lower level that you feel you really deserve.

One Taste of Freedom and You'll Never Be Satisfied With Less

Once I began to get a taste of freedom for myself, there was no turning back. I genuinely realized for the first time that the restrictions I had grown up seeing my parents labor under did not have to be my reality.

It was as though there had been an imaginary line drawn around me. I had accepted the idea that it was my lot through example and inheritance to not be allowed or capable of going beyond the circle in which I had seen my family and friends live their entire lives.

Once you get a taste for enjoying life, experiencing freedom, knowing that the BEST relationships, experiences and things are available to you—and not just available but waiting for you to show up to receive what is rightfully yours—there's no stopping you. **Sometimes the only reason that some people don't enjoy the best is that they just don't show up in life to claim what is theirs!**

I remember the first time one of my mentors took me to a five-star restaurant to eat a fine meal and enjoy the atmosphere. Until that time, I had felt that a place like that was a terrible waste of money. But since that time, I have learned that money isn't just pieces of paper with pictures of dead presidents or beautiful artwork printed on it. It is a symbol of the energy, creativity and precious time we have invested in accordance with the principle of *"sowing and reaping,"* or *"giving and receiving."* Therefore, money is an outer result of your inner thoughts of abundance or lack.

Now, let me reiterate that there are no "big shots" or "little shots" in life; we are all precious, valuable and wonderful. In fact, many times an individual who is perceived as a "big shot" is really just someone who is out of town with an attaché case swinging from one's arm. If you saw people like this around their families, they may not strut their stuff so egotistically because their family members know who they really are!

So money in and of itself does not make anyone better or worse than the next person, but the lack of financial freedom can certainly keep people so concerned about their financial condition that they are also hindered from being free in the other areas of life.

I have used this quotation many times, and I really like it because I think it sums up a very important thought: "One of the greatest things that having plenty of money will do for you is to relieve you from having to worry about not having enough money!"

When agreeing to allow someone to be your mentor, you want to make sure that the person is living a wellrounded, balanced life. **The opportunities to expand your vision of the possibilities in life while in the presence of a mentor are by no means restricted to financial freedom. But a** mentor can enable you to see a higher level of freedom for yourself spiritually, mentally, emotionally, relationally, in persistence, in confidence, in creativity, and in a multitude of other facets that make up your dream-purpose-life.

I've eaten in hundreds of fine restaurants since that experience of dining with a mentor, and I have never felt guilty about it or unworthy of it one time. After all, if those restaurants and all of the other wonderful things in life are not here for us, then for whom are they here?

The main point here is that some of the things that you will learn and receive from a great mentor are the things that you aren't taught in a classroom and cannot learn by standard practice. If a person living down by the curb can have the rewarding experience of being a close friend or even an assistant to someone living on the mountaintop of life, it is much easier for that person down by the curb to see oneself at the very least getting up to the top of the telephone pole!

Gaining a Larger Vision

There are many aspects to the wonderful world of being mentored and being a mentor, but I want to keep our thoughts here consistent with the focus of this book. So let's look further at how a mentor helps you in your thought replacement daily program.

Obviously, you learn some practical how-to strategies and skills from a mentor, but that practical know-how will not work for you the same way it is working for your mentor until you begin to expand your vision. The principles and methods you learn from your mentor will only work for you to the extent that you can begin to see the bigger view of life that has enlarged their perspective.

It's like three people looking through three different holes in a wall. One person is looking through a hole the size of a pinhead, the second person is looking through a quarter-inch wide hole and the third person is looking through a basketball-sized hole. It's the same wall and the scenery is the same on the other side of the wall, but what a different perception those three people will have!

In the workplace today and in the past, many employers and managers have tried to get their workers to look through the pinhole or, at best, through the quarter-inch hole. The reason for this is to keep their employees in a place where they feel so lucky to have that particular job that they will work for less pay and put in more effort than a person who is not on a guilt trip. Many people are working just hard enough to keep from getting fired, and their employers are paying them just enough to keep them from quitting.

When I first got out of high school, I immediately got a job in a factory because my dad had always worked in factories. My first factory job was running a punch press. I would put a flat sheet of metal in the twenty-foot-high press; then there would be a loud KA-*boom* sound as that press would crash into the sheet of metal, leaving its imprint, and then another loud noise as the press snapped itself back to its upward position. I would then pull that piece out, set it aside and pick up another flat sheet of metal and put it in the punch press. Eight or ten hours a day of that repetition and, even with the benefit of earplugs, all of the KA-*boom*, KA-*boom*, KA-*boom* was still driving me crazy.

But I stayed in that job for two years before it occurred to me that maybe I could at the very least find some work that I didn't hate so much and that could even be a real stepping stone to get me closer to my dreams.

What employers don't always realize is that the people who work for them would give much more of themselves to their work if they knew that in some way it was going to help them realize their dreams. Whether people are working for you or with you as partners in business, they will always run harder, faster and stronger if they can see very clearly "what is in it for them."

This same principle applies in our families. You can either try to get your spouse or children to do something the right way by putting them on a guilt trip or by showing them what is in it for them and why it is in their best interest to make it happen in the strongest way possible. Guilt trips always cause resentment and, though you may get what you want in the short run, over the long haul you will lose.

So a natural benefit that you receive from a mentor is to go from the pinhole vision to the quarter-inch view, to the basketball-sized hole; and then eventually you can just knock the whole wall down flat.

This larger vision causes you to also expand your knowledge base. And let there be no mistake about it: **knowledge is powerful.**

Picture yourself standing on a platform in the dark; you can't see how high the platform is above the floor. Now you take a step and feel yourself starting to fall off the platform. A large percentage of the terror you feel at that moment is due to the fact that you have no knowledge of how far you are going to be falling before you hit the floor.

Now, picture yourself on the same platform, but this time the lights in the room are on and you can clearly see that the platform is only six inches off the ground with a cushioned gymnastic mat lying right in front of you. Now, again, see yourself starting to fall off that platform. This time you become a little alarmed, but the feeling is not anywhere near the level of terror you felt in the dark.

What is the only difference in those two scenarios? In the latter paradigm, you simply have the benefit of additional knowledge. It is not an exaggeration to say that having one idea, reading one well-chosen book or listening to one targeted tape, can shift you from fear to faith, insecurity to security and shaky ground to solid footing. You will find that on most days you will receive more incredible ideas during a few hours spent observing your mentor than you would have been able to come up with over a long period of time operating with a trial and error approach.

Be a Mentor

Not only do we need to have a mentor that we are receiving from, but to perfectly align ourselves with the *"mentor principle"* we also must operate fully with the principle of *"reciprocity,"* which is the same as the principle that *"as you give, so you shall receive."* Therefore, along with having a mentor, we must also be mentoring someone else. Wherever you find yourself in life, there are people who need to rise up to the level that you are now on.

There are tremendous benefits to being a mentor. Just as you will probably be serving your mentor in some useful way, your protegé will most likely come to you with some talent or ability that will aid you in going after your dream-purpose. At the same time, you will be helping her or him go higher as well. Also, one of the best ways to learn more deeply about any principle and to plant more good thoughts in your daily thought replacement program is to teach those same principles as you are mentoring others.

A wonderful example of how this *"giving and receiving"* principle works is found in the comparison of two bodies of water in the Middle East.

The first part of the example is the Dead Sea. This sea has an inlet, which receives water, but no outlet to feed water into another body of water. Therefore, the sea has become stagnant and the salt content in the water is so high that the living creatures and plants you find in other seas, lakes and rivers cannot live there; thus the name the Dead Sea.

The second part of the example is a body of water in the Middle East called the Sea of Galilee. It has an inlet and an outlet, as most bodies of water do. Therefore, historically life has been abundant and flourishing; it has had a reputation of sustaining the life not only within its banks but also the animals and humans many miles around its borders.

Here is the principle found in comparing these two examples. *Giving creates a flow* that allows your best to come to you. Conversely, stingy, closed-off people always miss their best. It can get stuck downriver with not enough current for its transport. Even if it does reach them, it dies in the acidic, toxic water of their negative thoughts.

So be open to give, even when you have to believe in people before they begin to believe in themselves. There are few rewards in life that compare with sharing tears of joy with someone who has had a breakthrough when you know that you were instrumental in the guidance and mentoring that helped the seeds of their greatness take root and grow. You cannot flow in inspiration to help someone else without having that inspiration affect your thoughts and life in a positive way. Role models are a powerful influence, and there are few feelings of satisfaction like seeing someone duplicate the success that you have experienced as a direct result of your mentoring.

We all have been greatly affected by role models, whether we realize it or not. I remember watching public speakers when I was seven or eight years old. Then I would go into my bedroom as soon as I got home and shut the door. Sometimes I would grab a hairbrush; other times I would grab a pop bottle and hold it upside down: these would become my microphones. I would stand using my bed as a podium and speak to imaginary crowds of thousands of people. Deep down in my heart I believed that what I was doing was a practice run for what I would really do in the future. Even though an onlooker might have said, "Isn't that cute? What a far-fetched fantasy," I was only responding to my heart's urge to begin to let my purpose flow, even though it would still be years before the people would show up to listen!

Another very valuable thing to know about finding a mentor, working with a mentor and also being a mentor, is that great mentors are always great talent scouts. You will not find a great mentor messing around too long with a protégé who is not really serious about learning and growth. Though you could meet your next mentor while you are purchasing your next cappuccino, great mentors are not sitting around the coffee shop looking desperately for their next student; in fact they are probably not looking at all. The way it usually happens is that you catch their eye and get their attention because of your hunger, passion and desire to be the best you can be. This causes them to see themselves in you and brings back memories of when they were at the same place of growth that you are presently at.

They know that you are a good candidate because you are operating with the same mindset that has grown in them to take them to the higher, breakthrough levels and has been a catalyst for critical mass in their own journey to greater freedom.

As you are given the privilege of being with your mentor, "be a sponge" without "being a leech." Remember to respect your mentor as your teacher, but also be sensitive to his or her need for privacy and space as you would for any true friend.

For the period that you have been allotted time to be with your mentors, watch and observe everything you can without being too imposing on their goodness. Find out what books they read and tapes they listen to, what personal and professional habits are a part of their daily program, how they balance their work and family life, how they feed themselves spiritually and the list goes on and on.

There will be plenty of time to rest or give your attention a break later. While you are in the sphere of activity of a great mentor, be sure that you are alert and on the lookout at all times. The seemingly small nuances that you pick up from your mentor can color your life with much rich texture.

I remember one of my mentors teaching me the difference between *"nervous excitement"* and *"relaxed intensity."* Wow! What a difference there is!

Nervous excitement is a good place to start and usually is the first phase you go through when you start a project or endeavor.

But when it comes time to enroll other people in your vision to assist and support you, you will need to shift to *relaxed intensity.* **If real people of substance are going to enroll in your cause, vision or business, first they will have to be able to truly feel safe and secure with you and your vision or project.**

Relaxed intensity is obviously not a matter of sitting back in your easy chair doing nothing, or being laid back with no sense of urgency. Rather, it is a byproduct of working on your thoughts until you have settled it once and for all that you will see the vision come to pass no matter what it takes. While you will probably be moving with an increased sense of urgency and sometimes very similar outward activity, you will move beyond being tentative. Even the nervousness that you still have will be transmuted into a resolve of total commitment that supercedes any anxiety normally associated with moving beyond a comfort zone. When you "relax" the tension that comes from knowing that you may quit, give up, sell out or surrender your purpose, from that point on you no longer have to "try" to prove to anyone that you are "for real"; you exude only confidence.

We all love to feel safe and secure. When people <u>know</u> that they are standing on solid ground when they are standing with you, this "<u>knowing</u>" will cause you to become a magnet for the right people to connect with you and provide all of the support and assistance that you may need.

Become a Great Artist

I also picked up an amazing secret to another mentor's success. He was a master artist—not an artist with a paintbrush and canvas; he was an artist who painted beautiful pictures with words. I watched with amazement as he would talk to people either on the phone or in person. I could see how individuals were initially hesitant and suspicious about his new proposals, but within a matter of minutes they would draw closer and closer until they would voluntarily respond with finality in their voice and be compelled to ask him, "How can I be a part of what you are doing?" Many times this would all happen totally unsolicited on his part and usually before he had even had a chance to mention that he might consider letting them get in on his project. He had a constant support group of people around him who would fight any odds to bring the collective vision and dream to fruition.

I remember him telling me, "Larry, you have to become a great artist with words. Language and communication are the key. **You need to become so good at painting pictures with words that by the time you are done talking, people will be longing for you to paint them into the beautiful picture that you have created."**

This works in business and in your family life, as well as in other areas of your sphere of activity. You can either try to get people with a temporary lure of immediate gain, which will convince them to assist you for a day; or you can paint a wonderful picture of the rewards that come from delayed gratification, which will cause them to want to give their support over "the long haul."

Many a man has gone through this exact process, finding amazing creativity and inspiration to paint an incredibly convincing picture to show his sweetheart how wonderful their life will be together. When he feels that he has painted it well enough and with the most vivid colors and contrasts, then and only then does he pull out the diamond ring and have the confidence to ask the love of his life for her hand in marriage.

These kinds of lessons can be missed if you are not watching your mentor carefully, and I have found that mentors don't always bend over backwards to make sure that you get what is needed out of the example they are showing you. Many mentors can even seem abrupt or not really concerned with whether you "get it" or not. It's almost as if they know that if you "get it" too easily it probably won't stick or make a strong enough impression anyway. Some of the subtlest things that are "taught" or "caught" while in their presence could be the seed for one of your major breakthroughs in the future.

An Unbeatable Team

If we are still breathing, then we probably still need a mentor. **Down through the ages, the student-teacher relationship has perpetuated the greatness that would have been lost if it had only been written about in books or talked about by enamored onlookers.** The transference of the great secrets of the ages, both spoken and unspoken, have not only been preserved over the years but have grown more vital with each successive mentor-student generation.

The *"mentor principle"* will never go out of style. It doesn't matter how many high-tech communication tools we may acquire: nothing will ever replace the quality of two people being able to look each other straight in the eyes and share principles and experiences with a sincere desire to learn, grow and reach higher levels of purpose and freedom together.

As you serve others as their mentor, you will be pushed up higher as a result of taking their hands to help them go higher. As you stay in the presence of your mentor and stay teachable, constantly valuing the time that you are given to receive from your mentor, the potential for rapid and effective true, principle-based thought replacement to occur in you is unlimited.

One day spent observing a great mentor can propel you in the pursuit of renewing your mind, change your outlook on life and perpetuate the absorption and assimilation of the right way of thinking with more intensity than years of trying to learn the "way things work" as a loner endeavoring to reinvent the wheel. A great mentor is a great friend and a wonderful gift.

Chapter

6

The Power of a Daily Program

Your mind will be like its habitual thoughts; for the soul becomes dyed with the color of its thoughts.

—Marcus Aurelius

Motivation can change your day for the better. The habit of thoughts that inspire will change your life for the best.

—Larry DiAngi

A major part of my purpose for writing this book is to be able to deal in an expanded way with several points and principles that I have touched on very briefly in my previous works. Each time I speak at an event or write a book, I try to be sensitive to the needs of the people with whom I am communicating. One of the ways that

I know what areas of this message are meeting people exactly where they live and are also meeting that greatest needs in their lives is by the questions that people ask me. When I notice that individuals who live in many different geographical locations and lead very different lives are continually asking the same exact questions, I know that I need to focus in on those specific aspects of the message.

In response to the previous works that I have written, recorded or presented in live presentations and on my Internet Web site, one topic is at the top of the list. It could be in a letter, an e-mail, a telephone call or in person, but what ever the mode of communication I always love to hear someone ask me about "The Daily Program." This program is very dear to me because it has brought me through many trying times and also makes the good times even better. Many times I give forty-five minute talks, and I know there is no way that I will have enough time to explain this program completely. But while I am sharing other principles with the audience, I will just mention this program in passing and how it has changed my life. Immediately, I see people's eyes light up as they are listening to me, and I know exactly what they are thinking. The need for this type of approach to thought replacement is obvious.

Whether the questions about this topic are in writing or are asked of me personally, they usually go something like this: (1) "Larry, what is the daily program that you refer to so often?" (2) "What are the specific components to the program?" and (3) "How does it work?"

Believe me, I know the power of this simple daily program. I am certain of its incredibly positive effect in my personal and professional life, and I am always happy to share it with anyone who is interested.

Educated in the "University of Adversity"

I began to create this program over eleven years ago during the time when I was sleeping on the office floor. I had no outer reason to believe that I was destined for a dream-purpose of any kind. In fact, my circumstances seemed to be speaking very loudly to me that I had made some of the worst decisions of my entire life. The way my outer circumstances looked at that moment seemed to indicate that I had exercised some very bad judgment by leaving my ABC affiliate TV show, five-day-a-week radio program and local speaking arena to move to Detroit to launch my national speaking business. It appeared as though I had made a fatal move that had resulted in losing the dream I had been pursuing for many years.

I got very down on myself for a while and felt like a total fool for believing that the higher level I was going for was anything more than an insane vision of grandeur.

Learning to Fly Above the Turbulence

I came to a crossroads where **I had to decide which perspective I was going to take on my situation. I had two views to choose from. I would have to decide whether I believed that the circumstances were bigger than my dream-purpose or that my dream-purpose was too big to be stopped by my present circumstances.** Did I have really bad luck, or was I simply going through what most people experience while pursuing their dreams? After all, an eagle cannot fly without the resistance of air under its wings.

I began to consider the possibility that maybe this turbulence in my life could actually in some strange way help me to fly higher. I looked at Les Brown, and I knew for sure that one way or another he was going to pull himself out of the similar and even more precarious situation that he was in. I had also read countless books and heard many testimonials of stories of individuals who had fought "the good fight of faith" and triumphed over adversity.

So I set out to find a way to make my inner vision for the future stronger than my present circumstances. At first, I tried to just get motivated and pull myself up by the bootstraps, but this had a very temporary effect on me. I would find myself getting down many times each day, and the different techniques I was using to motivate myself seemed to be unreliable; they would only get me through shorter and shorter periods of time, until they lost their effect altogether.

I knew there had to be something deeper than just staying excited about reaching my goals. Then I began to go back and take another look at stories I had read and heard of examples of those who had created breakthroughs in their lives. I looked carefully at these examples to find the common thread in all of their stories.

I had obviously read and heard these stories before, but I had always looked at them with my concentration on the outer results these people were achieving. After taking a second look, I began to realize I had overlooked the inner work that they were constantly involved in to continue to press forward to achieve their dreams.

Through much research, I began to discover that the overwhelmingly consistent similarity in all of their cases was the way they thought. Most of these people were at times perceived by others to be a little odd because they seemed to live in a thought world way ahead of their outer circumstances and far beyond what they could prove in hard, cold facts to be their true destiny in life.

Then I ran across the principle that *"as it is within, so it will be without."* This is the sister principle to *"as your faith is, so it will be unto you"* and *"as he or she thinketh, so they shall be."*

I then began to realize that I had indeed created my own struggles by trying to force things to happen on the outside without changing who I was on the inside.

The Inspiration of Desperation

It was at this point of realization that I found myself in a similar mindset and "heartset" to the one I had been in about ten years earlier when I had taken my very first baby steps towards my dream-purpose. I was so desperate for what was *really real* that I was open and willing to move beyond my superficial ego and pride to lay myself on the "alter of change."

The point of surrender to your purpose is wonderful, for it is there that all the pretense, self-deception, resistance to change and fear of what other people will think about you will go right out the window. All you are left with is a sincere desire for that which is 100 percent real, and you have no interest in messing around with playing head games with yourself or others.

The Day and Night Principle

During this time in which my outer circumstances seemed to contradict the vision I was holding for my life, I found that the hardest times to stay centered were first thing in the morning and as I was trying to go to sleep at night. I made a conscious, deliberate effort to not leave those times to chance but to always keep a tape of someone speaking or music playing and to read an inspiring book every day without fail during those extremely vulnerable morning and evening periods.

Though I had read many times about the *"meditating day and night"* principle, I had never really recognized it for what it really is. Then I began to see this principle everywhere I looked, and I knew I was onto something big!

I was no different than anyone else in the sense that I did want my circumstances to improve. If you asked anyone on the street, "Would you like your life to be filled with increased freedom, love, prosperity—with less stress and more happiness?" the answer would most likely be yes. Just about everyone wants his or her life to be better.

But the challenge is to be able to stay on track during all of those days while you are still sowing, watering and fertilizing the seeds in your dream-purpose-garden without seeing any tangible evidence of your desired surface results. This period of time will put you to the test.

During this time of my personal testing, this daily program was conceived in my life experience. Little did I know it, but out of the ashes of what appeared to be my biggest failure would emerge a daily program that is now being used by individuals across the United States and in many other countries around the world.

While this approach was being formed through my experimentation with different techniques (which I now know to be methods for effective thought replacement), at that time I thought I was just doing whatever it took to get through the day without becoming depressed. I have since found that the need in our lives for this type of a program goes far beyond just using it long enough to get out of a jam or get unstuck. When practiced as a continuum, it is even more effective to help you to avoid getting into a stuck place to begin with; its major benefit is that it improves the quality of any day.

Over the years, I have tailored and tightened this daily program to increase its potency in my own life, and you can do the same. At the end of this chapter, I am going to give you an outline of the individual modules of this daily program for thought replacement. You may be tempted to turn to the end of the chapter to look at the program outline, but it probably will not make as much sense to you now as it will if you continue reading and arrive naturally at the end of the chapter. So I encourage you to resist that temptation, and keep on reading.

Over the years, I have made this program more concise and user-friendlier. What I will give you in this chapter is a boilerplate version that you can tailor to your personal needs and lifestyle. No two people share the exact same lifestyle, challenges or dream-purpose. But in the last eleven years, I have never met anyone who has not been able to tailor this program for one's own life and gain wonderful results if he or she is consistent with the steps given and committed to going to the next higher level.

Have a Big Why

In all things, the *why* is always more important than the *what*. *Why* you want to practice this program will be the driving force behind your persistence and relentlessness in staying on with continual thought replacement and not falling off into old patterns of thinking and doing.

The same kind of momentum builder applies here as it does in relation to being committed and successful in a physical fitness program. Why do some people discipline themselves to be faithful to a program of health, fitness and exercise, while others don't? It is because the ones who do succeed make being physically fit a part of their lifestyle and they find a way to stay continually focused on <u>why</u>

they are putting forth the effort. Individuals with this type of mindset are not looking for immediate results or instant gratification; they are in it for the long haul. They reject the whole notion that there is a "quick fix" or "magic pill" that will transform them into perfectly fit specimens.

Most people stay faithful to a fitness program for bigger reasons than just improving how they look. In fact, they begin to enjoy, appreciate and value how much better they feel even more than how good they may look. Through benefits of increased stamina and the good feeling of looking in the mirror at a fit person, individuals begin to feel more confident and find it easier to maintain a better attitude.

It is in this kind of process that we become very aware of the fact that the most wonderful thing occurring is not the act of reaching the goal. In fact, **reaching the goal often becomes secondary and the benefit that we value the most is *who we are becoming* in the process.**

The narcissistic quest is very shallow and unfulfilling at best, and it leaves one with greater feelings of insecurity as one travels further down that road. But if a person has the right *why* for a physical fitness program, then one fact is crystal clear. The added strength and stamina enjoyed physically, is, as in any worthy pursuit, simply an outer byproduct of the strength and vitality growing on the inside.

Give Your Mind a Physical Advantage

All that being said, a daily physical exercise program is an indubitable benefit and can even be a lifesaving habit. Regular, systematic physical exercise will improve the quality of your life and help regulate your weight, and it is a vital lifestyle ingredient to keep your heart and every other part of your body strong and resilient.

If you don't invest a little time now for physical fitness, then someday in the future you may be forced to take a lot of time to deal with the problems that result from such an oversight. One man said, "If I had known I was going to live this long, I would have taken better care of myself!"

This realization is not a new revelation to most people. Though many people still choose not to heed the warnings of the experts concerning the urgency for a physical fitness regime, more people today look after their health and reap the rewards of the life-changing effects of this simple discipline.

I must include here, before moving on, that your physical fitness definitely influences your mind in a positive or negative way. A person can be unfit physically and still be pretty sharp mentally, but why not gain the increased positive mental remuneration for having a stronger heart and a better flow of oxygen to your brain? Then add to that the increased stamina, decreased stress level, more flexibility, higher level of physical resiliency and a host of other paybacks that you will receive from adding this discipline to your lifestyle.

Just as individuals commonly put off starting a physical fitness program until "tomorrow" (a code word for an undercover operation of carefully crafted excuses and procrastination), people frequently neglect starting a fitness program for their thoughts. It is even more alarming to realize that the average person lives unconscious of the fact that a health program for one's thought life is even an option to consider, let alone become aware that the daily renewing of one's thoughts is a vitally important necessity.

Think About What You Are Thinking

We all go through pretty much the same phases in respect to our thought life. It seems that as the years click by, every individual to one degree or another picks up a fair amount of excess baggage in the form of debilitating thoughts. As we acknowledged earlier in this book, psychiatrists and psychologists have said that 87 percent of the average person's self-talk is negative on a daily basis.

Yet the "average person" is probably not even aware that he or she is thinking thoughts at any given moment! It is true that most people do not think about what they are thinking.

Still more amazingly, it seldom dawns on the average person that his or her thoughts at any given moment are very possibly not "their thoughts." Someone may say, "Wait a minute, Larry. If a person is thinking a thought, it must belong to that individual or he or she wouldn't be thinking it to begin with."

Well, let's examine this for a minute. Is it possible to receive a concept or idea from another person or from the media, education, et cetera, and just hitchhike along with that thought without ever really checking it out to see if it is true or good for your thought life? Of course, this is possible. Therefore, our minds can be filled with a lot of thoughts that we do not even know to be true, let alone healthy or profitable for us.

Living on borrowed thoughts can cause a person to feel like an impostor. The only thoughts that you can truly count on are the ones that you have proven to be true. There are no guarantees when we put ownership on random thoughts that we have not first qualified.

We have all, at one time or another, opened a container of milk or an item of food from the refrigerator and WAM! this awful smell hits us in the nose. Knowing that this particular food substance has gone bad, we would never dream of taking a big gulp or bite of it.

We need to be just as selective with our thought life assimilation. Even the most thought-conscious person knows there is always room for growth in this area. It makes sense to examine our thoughts and then reject or immediately spit out the ones that are not healthy for us. By not taking anything for granted and always endeavoring to consider whether we have personally really proven a particular "way of thinking" to be true, we can circumvent most self-imposed "inner" stumbling blocks before they even become an "outer" problem.

Whose Thoughts Are You Thinking?

As I mentioned earlier, another aspect of staying constantly aware of the quality of our thoughts necessitates that we take a look at the possibility that many of what we consider our thoughts are really other people's thoughts. One reason we can so readily accept these alien thoughts is that, for the most part, we end up thinking them in "the first person." In other words, we hear ourselves thinking these unqualified thoughts in our own voice and not in the voice of the person from whom we originally received them.

When we just accept a way of thinking at face value, that collection of thoughts affects us; and the results may, much to our dismay, cause us to lose ground rather than moving forward.

While there are thoughts that we "own" without qualifying them, there are also thoughts that I call "floaters." The peculiarity about "floater" thoughts is that while we never made an effort to do what was necessary to either "own them" or "reject them," these thoughts can keep us in a state of limbo and cause us to be indecisive.

These "pending" thoughts can definitely feed a person's tendency to procrastinate. As long as the "floater thoughts" are allowed to hang out in the ether around our head, we live in a state of feeling like we still have to wait for all the facts to come in before we can make a decision. These thoughts could by chance be healthy, but it is always risky business to allow them to continue swimming around on the surface of our mind without knowing what adverse side effects they may have.

Medication is a classic metaphor here. No drug is ever supposed to be released for the general public's use until the known possible side effects have been thoroughly researched and evaluated.

Some studies seem to indicate that we start receiving our first thought-forming influences while we are still in the womb. We all got here the same way: through a miracle of creation, we were conceived in our mother's womb; and within weeks we started hearing sounds coming to us from outside our warm, watery home. We may not have understood the language yet, but we could sure pick up whether it felt positive or negative. When there was a lot of loud noise and excitement in the yet unseen outer world, our little heart would start to beat faster. When we felt the vibration of soothing music via a sound system filtering through our mother's belly, our heart would slow down and we would become calm. We spent nine months in this secluded atmosphere and then BOOM... out we came.

Now we could assume that at birth a newborn baby starts out with a "clean slate" in his or her thought life. But that little bundle of joy may have already picked up impressions and feelings that will become a reinforced way of thinking. This can occur when the baby's five senses confirm what that sound or feeling was that they first heard or sensed while it was still muffled and hidden from view.

And so begins the process of absorbing endless messages that will begin to form our true, principle-based self-talk and our false, negative self-talk. Then we go through our early years of life soaking up new thoughts like a sponge.

We may have looked up to our parents as though they were the all-knowing, infallible, final authority on every subject. When we were very young, we probably figured that our parents would only tell us what was truly good for us.

When we no longer considered ourselves youngsters, we may have started to see that some of what our parents told us or demonstrated for us was not exactly "the way it really is." We were faced with other authority figures who seemed to be so credible that they were beyond scrutiny.

Yes, even as we progress through our adult years, the beat goes on and on. When we hear someone make a statement on a television news program or get some information or statistics off the Internet, much of the time we are led to believe that it must be true.

Well, we all realize that it is not quite that simple or clean-cut. We realize that every word and report we hear or see is not necessarily accurate but may fit into a collection of erroneous thoughts, and still may seem very logical when it is coming from what we believe we have proven to be a trusted, reliable source. It would be nice if thoughts not founded on truth would have no effect on us. But it is not the thought that has the power over us; it is our allowing the thought to take root and grow that brings about the birth of its offspring in our life.

One day, three young children were playing in the living room of their home. It was a cold, windy, winter day outside; therefore, indoor activities were the chosen form of entertainment for the day. Their parents had built a roaring fire in the fireplace that created a cozy atmosphere in contrast to the inclement weather that was visible through the icy windowpane.

The children began playing a game in which they would take turns being blindfolded and a random item would be placed in the blindfolded child's hands. The object of the game was for the blindfolded child to guess what the item was in ten seconds with only his or her sense of touch as a guide.

The first object was a paperweight, which the first child failed to guess correctly. The second was a piece of cardboard, which the second child successfully identified in six seconds. Then the third child took his turn being blindfolded. His brother removed a piece of ice from a nearby glass of pop sitting on the end table. As a joke, before the sibling put the ice in his brother's hand, he quickly said, "Here is a burning piece of wood from the fireplace" and then proceeded to drop the piece of ice into his brother's awaiting palm.

The sad conclusion to this story is that, just minutes later, the children's parents had to rush the young boy—the last blindfolded participant of that guessing game—to the hospital. He had received a second-degree burn in the palm of his hand exactly where the piece of ice had touched him.

The young boy believed the words of his brother, and tragically his mind and body reacted as though the object were truly a piece of burning wood.

The same type of phenomenon is also possible in a positive sense. There was another family who had two children: a son named Michael and a daughter named Melissa. The son seemed unusually bright for his age, so his parents had his IQ tested. The results from the test were proof that their son had an IQ high enough for them to expect him to become close to another Albert Einstein.

Not wanting to make their daughter feel inferior, they would never use Michael's name when referring to their "gifted child" in conversations with family or friends. They would just say something like "We have a very gifted child with an extremely high IQ." Their daughter always assumed that she was the one who had been bestowed with this incredible blessing and never said anything to draw attention to herself because she didn't want her brother to feel bad.

The years passed, and one day she took a lunch break and left the courthouse where she was a judge presently presiding over a trial of two corporations engaged in a lawsuit. As she left the courthouse, she passed by the office where she had previously worked as the district attorney. She had three inventions in the process of receiving patents and had recently finished writing a novel, for which a publisher had agreed to give her a $200,000 advance plus backend royalties. She thought to herself, "Life is good," as she drove to her mom's house for lunch with a feeling of satisfaction that she seemed to have had for as long as she could remember because of her many accomplishments.

While she was eating a delicious helping of her mom's homemade cooking, the phone rang. Her mother got up from the table and answered the phone with her predictably cheery, high-pitched "Hello!" On the other end of the line was her son, Michael, who was very depressed because he had just been turned down for a job at the local supermarket as a clerk, for which he would have had to start as a bagger.

Michael was now forty-six years old, and Melissa was forty-seven. Michael's mom, in an attempt to cheer him up, said these words: "Don't worry, honey. That job wasn't good enough for you anyway. Ever since you were young and we found out you were a gifted child, I have always known that you wouldn't be able to work at a boring job like that. You need to find work that is more challenging and use your genius for something worthwhile."

After her mother hung up the phone, Melissa, with a look of disbelief, asked her mother, "Did I hear you correctly when you were talking on the phone with Michael? Did you tell him that he was a gifted child?"

"Yes," responded her mother. "We had Michael tested when he was young and found he had an incredibly high IQ."

Still stunned by this late-breaking news flash, Melissa, with her jaw in a dropped position, finally was able to speak after several minutes of silence. "But, Mom, every time I heard you refer to your 'gifted child' while I was growing up, I assumed that you were talking about me."

With that, her mother responded with a chuckle, "No, honey. You were just a normal child in every way! In fact, sometimes it seemed that you had to try much harder than the other kids your age did just to keep up with them in your academics."

Melissa had seen herself as gifted and had meditated on those thoughts day and night for years, and she had ended up fulfilling that personal prophecy.

The truth is that we are all given special gifts and talents, but very few people ever collect the right thoughts that will allow them to conceive the reality of their own greatness. People would be able to manifest the possible outer results if they only knew their true specialness.

Then, of course, there are those who seem to have many strikes against them but keep getting back up from one defeat after another until they break through into a glorious crescendo of amazing accomplishments.

In the final analysis, it is not what happens to you in life that is most important; it is what your self-talk will allow you to do with what happens to you that determines the outcome. You can be like the cream that always rises to the top if you do what is necessary to keep your heart and mind full of the kind of thoughts that belong at the top.

Break Through the Resistance

As I proceed throughout the remainder of the chapter to lay out for you the pattern you can use for your own daily thought replacement program, keep in mind that the progressive shift in your thinking will occur in layers. Just as we have built layer upon layer to create the existing thought system that we are presently operating with, what we are now looking to implement is not a one-week or one-month fix-it program but rather an ongoing assimilation and elimination process.

As I mentioned earlier, we all begin picking up impressions and feelings even while in the womb; and then once we are born, the slate of our mind and heart continues to be filled with positive, true, nourishing thoughts and negative, false, toxic thoughts. This collection of thoughts has a controlling influence on every decision we make and determines our overall outlook on life as a whole and in specific situations and relationships.

When we understand that most people are not consciously aware of their thoughts, it is no wonder that people can go through life without ever becoming alarmed about the precarious condition of their thought life. Without being conscious of the need for thought replacement, they just roll from one thought to another like a ship without a rudder.

This program will help you turn on the lights in your thought life. At first, you may feel resistance from your old thinking patterns and habits. I encourage you to push through this initial feeling of going against the grain and work your daily program, even if you have a challenge disciplining yourself as first. An unwillingness to push past old thought patterns is one of the major reasons that most people get stuck in the place of living unconsciously in relation to their thought life and go through life on "automatic."

Each day that goes by fueled by further procrastination is one more day in which, out of the 40,000 to 50,000 thoughts assimilated in the average person's mind, only a small percentage of positive, "conscious" thoughts come and a majority of "automatic-unqualified thoughts" are added to one's philosophy and reality.

For the average person, being on "automatic" is kind of like being tuned in to two radio stations at the same time. The average person's thinking process is tuned in such a way that one hears the wrong channel much stronger than the right channel, in addition to a lot of mental and emotional static.

Automatic-Positive Versus Automatic-Negative

We were not created to have negative thoughts be automatic. This is a learned trait. Many people gravitate toward the negative because they have been taught that the downside is more probable than the upside.

As you move along with the thought replacement program, which I will now lay out for you, you will immediately begin to replace old, automatic, debilitating thoughts with new true, principle-based thoughts. And that's great, but something even more wonderful is happening as an overall result of this process. Over a period of time, as you consistently work this program in your everyday life, you will notice that the positive self-talk will become your predominant "automatic" way of thinking; you will actually begin to repel the majority of negative self-talk before it has had a chance to affect you.

So as you launch into thought replacement, don't let the resistance of your negative self-talk throw you off course with the feeling that you are being "too positive." Other people may give you the impression that they think you are being too high-minded because you won't wallow around in negativism, but they will also notice that you have an increasingly attractive energy about you.

The common way of thinking cannot hold us back if we know that its whole foundation is false and its resistance is only temporary.

I work this program in my life every day, and I am so excited to share its simplicity with you. Using this program, you can open up a whole "new world" of possibilities for your life and be exhilarated with an overall experience of being renewed every day to go forth with purpose to be who you were born to be.

The Program

On the last pages of this chapter is an outline, as well as

more ideas that you can use while you are developing and tailoring your own daily thought replacement program.

The daily program begins before you get out of bed in the morning and concludes each night as you are drifting off to sleep.

The first module in the program consists of a series of *morning reality check statements.* You begin to use these *reality check statements* as soon as your alarm has sounded or the moment you are aware that you are no longer fully asleep.

Each of us has a moment like this every morning when one is in a state of not being fully asleep and not yet fully awake. This transitional state each morning is a very vulnerable time for us as human beings. This time of going from sleeping state to waking state has been proven through research to be one of the most impressionable and, at times, the most impressionable time of a person's day. The guards and the checks-and-balances system we usually access to decide whether we will or will not accept any given thought are not yet working at an effective level. While in this state, we know that we are pretty much free of expected outside influences to deal with. And we are in a condition of mind much like the vulnerability that a person experiences when under the influence of various types of drugs that lower one's ability to make decisions properly.

Therefore, it is vital that you begin the discipline of this program even before you open your eyes in the morning. *This* transitional time period of each morning is the bridge you must cross in order to start your day.

The specific *reality check statements* you choose to use here are to be those that mean something powerful to you at this time in your life. It is good to make sure to include a good number of statements that plant true, principle-based thoughts that relate to areas of your life where you are experiencing restriction of any kind.

Remember the exercise I asked you to do in Chapter 4, in which you looked at the areas of your life and wrote either freedom or restriction next to each area. It would be good for you to refer back to that assessment and deliberately target the areas of restriction in your life with these morning statements. It is also an excellent idea to continue to place a good amount of your focus on those areas throughout this entire daily program. By doing this, you can also be sure that you are planting the right thoughts in the areas of your life where the highest percentages of negative self-talk are present.

As you are lying in bed in this not-fully-asleep and notfully-awake time of your morning, say whatever truth statements come naturally to you. These are a few of the statements that I use: *"I was born for a great purpose. No matter what happens today, I can handle it. I will live this day in peace, strength and abundance. This day is a gift, and I will not take its value for granted. Whenever it is possible, I will be a support and a blessing to the people I come in contact with. I purpose in my heart to be the best husband and father I can be. As I meditate and work in alignment with the right laws, I will prosper in whatsoever I do."*

You can feel free to use some of these, and I also encourage you to sit down with a pen and paper and create some of your own. You can also find many statements in books. Sometimes you are reading a book and a line jumps out at you. Go ahead and add that one to your list for the next morning. In fact, if you carry a pen and paper everywhere you go, you will be amazed at the gems you will be able to capture throughout the day. They can come from something written, from something you hear someone say, from a song that you hear and from many other sources.

You can say these statements to yourself silently or out loud, depending on which feels more natural to you and whether or not you are concerned about waking up someone else. I have found that, especially when I am going through times of intense challenge in my life, saying these statements out loud has more of an effect on me. But it's totally up to you to decide what works best for you.

The important thing is that you do not just lie there letting your mind wander, thinking about what you need to do that day, the problems that will need to be solved and even the things that you are happy about that day.

All of these things are temporary and can change. You can get up excited about taking a trip that day, and the plans can get cancelled. You can be filled with expectancy about buying a new house, and the people selling it could change their mind and decide to keep it. You can be happy about the support you are receiving from someone, and the person could be having a rough day and forget the promise to help you do something that you needed assistance with.

I don't mean to paint a dark picture here, but we all know that the only absolute that you really have the total ability to have in complete control is the Real You. So these morning mind wanderings that occur before you are fully awake are useless at best and deluding at worst. What you want to concentrate on is what *you know to be true* to set you on the right course for the day before your feet even hit the floor.

This entire daily program is nothing more than a systematic approach for choosing to focus your thoughts on the truth about the way you and your life were purposed to be. In no way are we trying to enter into a fantasy world where we detach from the present circumstances of life. *Where we are right now is where we are; and what it is, is what it is.*

If you have only $2.51 in the bank account, then it would be unwise to write a check for $251.00, unless you were sure that you would be able to deposit at least that amount before the check got to the bank.

If you know that you have not been pursuing your dreams with the resilient power of purpose, then *the way that it has been is the way it has been* and it doesn't do any good to candy-coat it. But from this moment forward, we all have an opportunity to begin to plant new thoughts that will make our future better than our past, regardless of how good or bad the different facets of our past may have been. Each new day is another opportunity to readjust our focus by working a daily program to plant new thoughts that will keep our life on target.

Being out of balance is unnatural, even though the people who do live a centered life are in the minority. The trick is to be able to walk through life every day encountering people who are not on target with their purpose and at the same time hold the vision of yourself totally <u>on purpose</u>. Even if we get a little off track, we are pulled back on focus by our "knowing" that living a centered life is more than just a good idea; it is the way it was meant to be for us.

No matter how far south you travel, when you turn around in the opposite direction you are going north. And no matter how far we have gone into the outer limits of negative self-talk and the outer self, when we turn around we are heading back home to the true life that is ours to enjoy. **It's all about getting back to the true way that our life is supposed to be and then progressively moving forward to realize and live the dream-purpose-life that is our destiny.**

The First Component Continued

Okay, let's get back to the first component of the daily program. As you are still lying in bed in the morning, at the very beginning stages of going from your sleeping to waking state, is a vitally important time to begin to say reality check statements to yourself. Here are a few more of the reality check statements I use and you can work with as well: *"I was born for a great purpose. My purpose is bigger than any problem that I may face today. I will invest this day into the growth fund of my dream. I will guard my heart, for out if it flow the issues of life. As I think this day, so I will be. I am transformed by the renewing of my mind. The percentage of negative self-talk that I have collected will be reduced today and replaced with true, principle-based thoughts. It is my right and privilege to go forth and create, subdue and recover all of the purpose that has been given to me to live. I will love and respect others today, without allowing them to manipulate me. I will make peace today whenever possible. I will live this day to maintain integrity with my purpose. I will be true, giving, loving, forgiving and supportive to my family and friends. Those who are not pleased with my pursuing my purpose with a passion are free to not agree with me without any effort from me to convince them against their will. I am loved today. My purpose is becoming clearer all the time. As I change my thoughts, I change my life. I plant this day as a seed in the soil of my dream-purpose, and it will bear much fruit as I continue to die to my old, negative self-talk and come alive to the real thoughts that I was created to meditate on. Whatever this day may bring, I realize that there are no accidents but will deliberately extract as much growth as possible out of every circumstance."*

As you do your reality check statements, it may seem as though you are rambling on—and that is exactly what you want to do. You want to *flow* in the thoughts that bring you strength and center you on that which is real and true. So don't be overly concerned about using perfect grammar or complete sentences. In this practice of thought exchange, IT TRULY IS THE THOUGHT THAT COUNTS! Even if you make a mistake and say something inaccurate, you can always go back and correct yourself by restating that thought again correctly.

Also, know that as you continue with this program, you will grow in clarity concerning different principles and truths. What you want to include in your reality check statements is the best of what you know at that point in time. If you receive more enlightenment that day, then you can include your newfound knowledge in your next reality check session. By spending only three, four or five minutes lying in bed saying these truths to yourself, it is very easy to plant sixty to one hundred new true, principle-based reality thoughts.

Since light is more powerful than darkness and truth is more powerful than error, as you continue to repeat what is true for you, it will become stronger and stronger. Truth replaces error in the same way that light replaces darkness in a room when you flip on the light switch. The thoughts you are assimilating will force the old, erroneous thoughts out and replace them with the truth about every area of your life. You will be strengthened spiritually, mentally, emotionally, relationally, financially and within an almost unlimited number of other areas and sub-areas of your life.

Sub-areas are the components that make up the major areas of your everyday life. To give you an example, let's take the area of being a great friend. If you look at the area of being a true friend, you will find that within this general area are specific sub-areas. Some of these sub-areas are as follows: being there for others when they need you; keeping in touch even in very busy times; forgiving them when you feel they have hurt you; asking for forgiveness when you know that you have let them down; giving to them at times when you know you should, even if you don't feel like it; knowing when to say no; not letting money become a blockage in your friendship; being thankful for their love, consideration and help; respecting their time with their spouse; giving them wise counsel when you feel that it will help; not giving them counsel when you sense that they are not ready to receive it; being a support to them in their thought replacement program; supporting them any way you can as they pursue their dream-purpose.

I have barely scratched the surface of all the possible sub-areas of "being a friend," but you can start to figure out which principles to apply to help in these different subareas. As you glance back over the sub-areas to being a friend listed above, you will find that some of them are enriched by specific principles, such as *"giving and receiving," "forgiveness," "thankfulness," "supporting as your want to be supported," "being nonjudgmental"* and the list goes on and on.

So when you plant the thought *"I will be true, giving, loving, forgiving and supportive to my family and friends today,"* you plant a thought that, as it takes root and grows, will in a positive way affect all of the sub-areas of friendship at one time. I am so glad it works this way because to deal with all the sub-areas of life separately would be impossible.

Planting these friendship thoughts will also sensitize you to see clearly those who are only pretending to be your friends with ulterior motives or those who may have certain enjoyable qualities but, as a whole, are in some way pulling you down.

The Second Component

Now, let's move on to the point when you've done your morning *reality check statements* and are now ready to get out of bed. The next segment of time in your daily program is to spend twenty minutes either reading a book or listening to a teaching tape or music. Depending on the amount of exclusive focus needed for the particular subject you are receiving, you may also be able to absorb the same quality of replacement thoughts by listening to teaching tapes or music while you are shaving, putting on your makeup or showering.

This twenty-minute dose of replacement thoughts, along with this entire program, is to be done in addition to all of the things you already do to stay spiritually and mentally fit. If you usually pray when you first get out of bed, then by all means do not change anything that you are already doing. If you already have a reading time in the morning, then also keep that the same as you do normally.

Everything that I am suggesting is to be done in addition to what you already do. This may require getting up twenty minutes earlier each morning. One may ask, "Why should I add another reading, tape-listening or music-listening time to my morning if I already read each morning?" It is because the purpose of this twenty-minute dose of thought replacement is to specifically target the areas that you are frustrated with, fearful about, restricted in or insecure about in your life.

When choosing what to focus on during this twentyminute morning session, it would be a good idea to again refer back to the exercise that you completed in Chapter 4. That exercise is a tool for you to accurately identify the areas you need to focus on with the most intensity. Throughout this entire program, a large percentage of your thought replacement focus should be geared toward any area that you wrote the word "restriction" next to. The word "restriction" is a general term that encompasses the feelings of fear, insecurity, unworthiness, depression, stress, lack, unforgiveness, frustration and gloom, along with a host of negative emotions.

So when you choose the book that you will read, the tape or music that you will listen to or any other thought replacement tool that you will consider for use during this twenty-minute morning session, make sure that you will be receiving positive, truth thoughts that will target the areas of life where you have the greatest need. Of course, as I mentioned, the areas in which you have the greatest need will also be the areas in which you also have the highest percentage of negative self-talk.

This twenty-minute segment may involve reading one day and listening to music another day and talking on the phone with a friend for encouragement the following day. The other reading that you normally do each morning and other similar activities are disciplines that I encourage you to continue because discipline is good and has an aggregate effect on you.

You could do your regular reading with the purpose of continuing to read a book straight through to the end, and some days it just doesn't seem to be as interesting to you but you keep reading it anyway. This daily thought replacement program serves a different purpose than your standard disciplines do. After keeping this discipline up for two, three or four days in a row, WAMO! you get the aggregate effect of those two, three or four days all at once!

There is nothing magical about the number of minutes—twenty or any other number—that I may suggest. This program does not need to be regimented with the exact number of twenty minutes each morning. One morning, you may invest fifteen minutes and another morning you may invest forty-five minutes. The important thing is that you do SOMETHING every day.

This segment of approximately twenty minutes of your morning is to be filled with something that you can feel working on the key areas where you know that you need thought replacement. If you are going through a lot of financial struggles, then take in some principles on prosperity. If you are dealing with feelings of unworthiness, then work on that. If you are having a hard time forgiving someone for something that he or she did to you, then take in some thoughts that reinforce the principle of *forgiveness*. If the need is in your relationships, then find good tools that feed you the laws for having great relationships. And so forth.

You have to trust your instincts as to whether you will choose to read, listen to a teaching tape or a music CD, receive encouragement on the phone or do another activity that will plant new truth thoughts in your mind. The way you know which approach to take on any given morning for this twenty-minute segment is to try them all out till one "sticks." I will pop a tape in, push play and know within thirty seconds if it is targeting what I need that particular morning. The same approach applies with a book, music and so forth.

Now, again, you have your disciplined times still in place in which you can press through and read or do whatever, whether it feels like you are getting anything or not. But this twenty minutes is spent receiving thoughts that you know are hitting the spot where you need them the most.

I would guess that your experience with tapes, music, books and other tools is similar to mine with respect to the inconsistency that I have noticed. One day I will read one paragraph out of a book, and whatever thoughts were in that paragraph hit me so hard that I am energized, centered and strengthened in an area where I need it the most. The next day I can read that same paragraph but it does very little for me, but that day a teaching or speaking tape hits me where I need it. The next day the books and the tapes don't hit the spot, but music does. The next day it is calling a friend for an uplifting conversation.

At first, the flexibility that you must exercise in this area can take a little getting used to. But over time, after you have worked with this program for a while, in most instances you will get out of bed and know exactly what tape to listen to or which source is right for that morning. At times, you will even know the night before and already have the book open or the tape or CD in the player waiting for you when you wake up.

The Third Component

So far, we've talked about the morning reality check statements and the twenty-minute session of thought replacement. The next module of the program is to take ten-minute doses of what I call "time-released information, inspiration and influence" throughout your day. We have all heard of time-released cold medicine or time-released vitamin C. Well, here we are taking time-released ten minute doses of renewing thoughts. Again, "ten minutes" is just a guideline; these doses could be two or fifteen minutes.

The information and inspiration for the most part will come from sources like books, tapes and music. The influence will most likely come from people. The influence from a friend, mentor or someone else who is also working on oneself and pursuing one's dream–purpose is the kind of influence that you are looking for. Even a simple two- or three-minute phone call can do the trick. Some days you may only need two ten-minute doses, and another day you may need twelve ten-minute doses!

How do you know when you need another ten-minute dose? Well, as with most principle-based approaches, this is a very simple thing to determine. The effect and approach for these ten-minute doses is very much along the same lines as what you want to accomplish in your twenty-minute sessions, except that these ten-minute doses are in response to a sudden need to get centered. You know you need another ten-minute dose when you are moving throughout your day and you notice that you have started to feel fear, insecurity, unworthiness, stress, neediness, anger or any other negative emotion. These feelings could occur in reaction to an obvious, specific stimulus; or you may not have a clue about why you feel the way you do. Whether you can pinpoint the cause or not is not the most important thing. What is most essential is that you do not allow your mind and emotions to continue down the wrong path.

Again, let's remember that our physical body, our mind, our will and our emotions are just "tools" that we have been given. These are all part of the outer self. The Real You was never meant to become a slave to your body, mind, outer will or the fluctuation of out-of-control negative feelings in your emotions. These outer-self "tools" are not bad in and of themselves—any more than an electric saw is bad; but if that electric saw is not controlled with a good intention, it can cause serious injury in an out-of-control state of operation. This applies in a direct parallel with the various dimensions and features of the outer self. These are all tools that you have been given to use, and you do not have to be controlled or used by them.

Therefore, when we get into a place of fear about something or someone, why should we live with that fear for hours or even days? Why not go get a ten-minute dose of some renewing thoughts that will take you from that place of fear and back onto a foundation of faith?

The only way that fear can show up is for us to drift out into negative self-talk. **If you can continue to know that you know that you know that you are *on purpose*, then you also will know that what people think about you or the way the circumstances seem to be at the moment are only temporary but your dream-purpose is permanent.**

On occasion people will come up to me after a seminar or after listening to my six-tape series titled *Own Your Dream* and will say, "Larry, you recommend that we take ten minutes of information, inspiration or influence every time we feel fear, insecurity or any other negative emotion; I have a problem with that. You see, I work a job with a boss who would frown on my sitting down to read or focus on positive thoughts when I should be working. How can I do what you are suggesting and not get in trouble with my employer?"

I believe that you should maintain integrity in every area of your life, and that includes not taking advantage of your employer. If you have agreed to give a certain amount of service each day with only scheduled breaks for free time, then do not violate the promise that you have made to your boss. But, just as there may be a designated place where you may take your scheduled breaks, there is also a room in most places of employment called the "restroom." Now why do they call it the restroom? Of course, your boss doesn't think of it as a place for you to go to rest and renew your mind, but whoever named it must have been thinking of some kind of rest when he or she labeled it!

Now I am being a little "tongue in cheek" here, and by no means am I saying to go in the bathroom stall and take a fifteen-minute nap. But I don't think there are many employers who would have a problem if one of their employees disappeared to the restroom two or three times a day for about three to five minutes each time. Just keep a pocket-sized book or an inspirational magazine article in your pocket or purse, go into the restroom stall and take a three- to five-minute dose of some good thoughts. You might even get lucky and be able to take care of your thought life and use that room for its other purpose at the same time.

If you do the type of work that permits you to listen to tapes while you are driving to an appointment or doing some kind of physical activity, then you are positioned very well for these ten–minute doses. Anymore, I don't even wait until I feel something negative. Whenever I have a free space in my daily schedule, I always pop in a tape or CD and press play. Not a day goes by that I don't listen to at least one tape and read something inspirational.

Through working this program over the years, I have developed an insatiable hunger for principle-based truth. For me, this craving is very similar to the craving for delicious food. I have developed a taste and a desire to receive the rich nourishment of principle-based laws and the truth that causes these laws to work. As you work with this program, you may also begin to develop this increased hunger on a continual basis. The need for this nourishment has been inside you all along, but through working with daily thought replacement you increasingly hunger and thirst after the right kinds of "eye and ear food" in the form of fortifying thoughts and ideas.

The Fourth Component

Along with your morning reality check statements, your twenty-minute morning dose and your time-released ten-minute doses, there is one more module to this daily program. It takes place as you are lying in bed getting ready to drift off to sleep. Based on the way this program flows, when I get to the place in a live seminar where I am about to share this fourth component, most people can usually guess what to do here before I even say it. Yes, that's right: you take some more of those reality check statements that you started your day with while you were waking up that morning. The last thoughts that you fill your mind with at night as you drift off to sleep are freedom, purpose-powered, strengthening thoughts.

It Gets Better All the Time

Wow! I have been working with this program for years, but I get more excited about its life-changing potential every time I have the opportunity to tell someone about it. The main reason I get so inspired when I explain it is that I know how well it works. What you create for yourself by faithfully working this program is an airtight day of thought replacement. Even before you are fully awake in the morning, and then all day long, and again at the close of your day as you are drifting off to sleep at night, you have been on a continuum of raising your level of positive self-talk and lowering your percentage of negative self-talk. You have also dealt with and disposed of fears, insecurities, anger and other toxic thoughts before they have had a chance to take root and grow.

Will this program completely change your entire life in one day? No, it probably won't. Will you be once and for all time totally transformed in one week or one month? No. We never get to the place where were have "arrived" and will stop benefiting from this kind of growth. But if you will tailor this program so that it will work with your particular lifestyle and faithfully keep at it every day, you will be amazed at what a difference a day or week can make.

I am not telling you that it is always going to be easy. There are many mornings when I am awakened by a wakeup call from the front desk of the hotel where I am staying while out of town for a speaking engagement. I pick up the phone and hear those familiar words on the other end of the line: "Good morning. This is your wake up call." After I search around with my eyes still shut and finally find the place to put that phone back on the hook, many times the last thing I feel like doing is saying reality check statements to myself. Many times, my body just wants to roll over and go back to sleep. I may have been traveling the night before and had delayed flights that caused me to arrive at the hotel at one or two o'clock that same morning.

My natural mind may be foggy and uncooperative, but I know from past experience that if I push through the first two, three or sometimes four minutes of resistance from my outer self, I then begin to feel my "knower" kick into gear. Though it is not necessarily easy to press through to that point, once I get there it is sure worth it.

We must make sure that our "knower" is turned on at all times. Your "knower" is the Real You and loves to feed on the right kind of thoughts. As you work this program, every day your "knower" is going to get stronger and the negative self-talk is going to get weaker.

Are you always going to feel like working your thought replacement program every day? Probably not. Will it be easier to keep at it once you start reaping the benefits? Yes, it definitely will. Will it be worth it if you don't quit, and will you be glad that you kept at it until it became an unbreakable habit in your life? ABSOLUTELY.

Daily Thought Replacement Program Quick Reference Outline

Module One

Morning Reality Check Statements

While you are still lying in bed going from the sleeping state to the waking state, say statements and phrases to yourself to plant true, principle-based thoughts. Continue to do this until you are fully awake; a minimum of four to five minutes is recommended. You can refer back to the two places in this chapter where I gave you some ideas for the kind of thoughts that you can plant during this morning session.

Module Two

Morning Twenty-Minute Focused
Thought Replacement Session

The key word here is *focused.* As I mentioned earlier in this chapter, none of this program is to replace any other reading or other disciplines that you have already set for yourself. This program is to be in addition to all of your other spiritual and personal development.

This twenty-minute session is to be filled with one activity. Find a source that you can receive thoughts from that strengthens you in the exact areas where you feel weak, fearful, frustrated, restricted, et cetera. One day a teaching tape will work for this session; the next day that same tape may not meet the need. Reading some of a book that is focused on the area that you need to renew your thoughts may work another day. Listening to music or making a phone call to a friend, mentor or someone else who is also working to renew one's thoughts and is pursuing one's dream-purpose is yet another possibility.

You can complete this twenty-minute session while getting ready in the morning, as long as the activity you are involved in does not require total concentration. Listening to a teaching or music tape or CD can effectively work for thought replacement while you are shaving, showering, putting on makeup and so forth.

The important thing is that during this twenty-minute period you are assimilating thoughts that are hitting you in the areas of your thought life where you need the most renewing. These areas are the ones in which you presently have the highest levels of negative self-talk and the greatest challenges.

Whatever the source for receiving renewing thoughts, whether a book, a tape or otherwise, you want to make sure that you can feel it working. Don't be afraid to keep experimenting until something starts working. If a book doesn't do the job for you one particular morning, then switch off to a tape. If the tape doesn't work, switch off to a phone call to a friend or mentor. If that doesn't "hit the spot," then try some music.

As you first get started with this program, it might be more of a challenge to find the exact right source each day. But after you stick with the program for a while, it will be first nature to know exactly what you need almost instantly each morning, and sometimes you will even know the night before what this twenty-minute session should consist of the following morning.

Module Three

Ten-Minute Time-Released Doses of Information, Inspiration and Influence

Ten minutes is just a guideline. These sessions can be two minutes or fifteen minutes, depending on what fits your schedule. One day you may need two of these doses, and another day you may need ten doses.

The *information* and *inspiration* will again most likely come from things like books, tapes, CDs and the like. The influence part will come from people. Of course, you can also receive information and inspiration while you are operating in the area of influence.

The way that you receive your renewed thoughts in this session is much the same as you will in your morning twenty-minute module, except this is in smaller doses. How do you know when you need another dose? You know when you need another dose when you begin to experience fear, insecurity, doubt, high stress levels or any other negative emotion.

Two to five minutes or even ten to fifteen minutes of this activity, if you can spare the time, will work wonders to stop the fear or other negative emotions before they have a chance to grow; and you can replace those thoughts with positive self-talk. You can refer back earlier in this chapter for more tips on how to best utilize these ten-minute sessions.

Module Four

Bedtime Reality Check Statements

Yes, that's right. You end your day the same way that you started it. The process of falling asleep is easier for some than it is for others. What usually happens at that time of your day is that your mind starts to wander and you start to think of the things that happened that day or possibly the things that you will need to do tomorrow. The strongest thoughts usually fall into two different categories: (1) the extreme joys of your life and (2) the tremendous challenges or concerns that you are facing.

How many times have you lain awake in bed unable to go to sleep because you were so excited about something wonderful that just happened or was about to happen? You could be leaving for a vacation the next day, which will take you to some amazing place for days of anticipated fun and enjoyment. The thought of this puts you in a state of euphoria, and the fact that you cannot fall asleep may not even bother you at all.

Then there are those times when the pressures of life twist your mind into knots and you go over and over them in your brain as you labor over an unresolved issue in your life. It may be something to do with a relationship struggle or challenge. It may be a concern about your work. It could be a financial dilemma that you can see no immediate solution for. It could be a feeling of guilt for something you said or did that day.

We all probably have lain there at one time or another and been haunted by something that we said to someone that day. We wish we could take back the words we spoke to the person. We are possibly concerned that our words were misunderstood.

We may go over and over the words someone else spoke to us that hurt us on a deep level or maybe something someone said that caused confusion in our mind and we are not exactly sure what was meant.

We could be contemplating a large purchase, such as a house or car, and all of the pros and cons with a slew of other details keep churning in our head like clothing in a washing machine.

The list of things we go to sleep thinking about is endless. Whether you are one of those people who go to sleep easily or one who has trouble shutting your mind down to fall asleep, the end result is still the same: you fall asleep with whatever your last thought was before you drifted off.

Some mornings in the past, you awaken with an unexplainable feeling of worry or concern, and other mornings you feel peaceful and confident without really being able to pinpoint why one morning feels so different than the last. A contributing factor to what determines how you feel when you wake up is your last thought as you fall asleep the night before. If you have trouble falling asleep, the quality and topic of your thoughts at night could be determining how much sleep you get; and we all know that sleep deprivation can impact our attitude and energy level the next morning, not to mention our overall outlook on life.

Some people can use sleep as an escape and are not usually kept awake by worries because this state of unconsciousness becomes their drug of choice; but, when they wake up the next day, all of those concerns hit them as soon as, or maybe even before, their feet hit the floor. Should we leave to random chance our thoughts as we fall asleep? The obvious answer is NO.

So, as you drift off to sleep, begin to say to yourself the same kind of uplifting, nourishing, true, principle-based thoughts that you awoke with that morning. The last thing on your mind each night is a series of creative, reassuring, renewing, regenerative, wonderful replacement thoughts. If you have trouble going to sleep at night, the reality check statements at bedtime very possibly may help you with that as well.

Well, there you have it. Now it's up to you to tailor this program to fit your lifestyle and make it something that you are going to stick with, no matter what it takes. It may involve getting up twenty minutes earlier every morning. But whatever it takes for you to make this work in your life, you are worth it. The morning and bedtime reality check statements alone are life-changing additions to a person's day. I have received many letters, phone calls and e-mails through my Web site that have confirmed the fact that this program will work wonders for anyone who will "work it" faithfully.

Reevaluate Your Other Thought-Forming Habits

There are many other things we need to consider in our daily routine that can greatly affect our thought life. For example, I have known people who can't fall asleep without the TV on.

I remember staying at the house of a married couple so that I would have a chance to visit with them while I was doing some business in the city they lived in. I was sleeping in their guestroom, or I should say I was <u>trying</u> to sleep in their guestroom. All night the TV was blaring away, and I could hear it clearly coming through their bedroom wall into the room I was staying in.

Bleary-eyed from my substandard night's sleep, I came down to the breakfast table the next morning and could not resist asking them, "Why did you guys stay up all night watching TV?"

They replied, "Oh, we weren't watching it. We just got used to it being on, and now we leave it on because we can't go to sleep when we don't hear the sound of the TV— it's just one of those things!"

After I left their house, I started thinking about that and remembered what I had learned about the subconscious mind. Even though a person is asleep, his or her subconscious is still receptive and registers the sounds and activity within hearing distance. That means every night that particular husband and wife were receiving thousands of random thoughts from whatever happened to be on TV throughout their sleeping hours. That is pretty scary when you think about it!

Another common, but not necessarily healthy, practice for one's thought life is using an alarm clock radio. In fact, even the word "alarm" is a little strange. Is that really the way we should wake up in the morning: alarmed and ready to tear the clock out of the power outlet and throw it at the wall? For the health and well-being of your thought life, I recommend that if you have a radio wake-up device you set it to a radio channel that is nourishing and uplifting. Even then, you are taking the chance of waking up to a commercial or a D. J. with the wrong attitude! What is even better is to buy a wake-up device that has a really nice-sounding beep to it, so that it gradually lifts you out of your sleep. I f you need something more to wake you up, then buy two of them and they can do a duet for you every morning! Of course, one of the nicest ways to wake up is to a tape or CD alarm clock; you can be brought from sleep-land to awakeland with the beautiful musical background of your choosing, which can also accompany you as you are doing your reality check statements.

Why am I going on and on about this sort of thing? Because much of our agitation, discomfort, frustration and stress in life is avoidable with sometimes just a few minor adjustments. At other times, some larger adjustments are necessary, but the improvement to our quality of life is certainly worth the changes that are minor in comparison. The different options for waking up or falling asleep are pretty simple choices to make. Unfortunately, many folks just don't stop to consider the atmosphere they are creating and the power of its influence on them for the good or for the bad. Remember the principle *"Guard your heart, for out of it flow the issues of life."*

When it comes to "things of the heart," one can even pick up the feelings of joy or disturbances from far away. This heart receptivity is not something spooky; it is just an amazing fact of the way we were made. You may have heard of someone (or you may have even had the experience yourself) waking up out of a sound sleep and having a feeling that someone the person knew was in trouble.

This used to happen with my mother and me all the time. I would come home one of those late nights during my early wayward years and the next morning at the breakfast table my mom would say, "Larry, what happened to you last night at about 11:00 P.M.?" When I thought back to that time frame, I would relate to my mother some instances and not others, depending on the nature of each activity. But let's just say that my mother nailed it almost every time. I was either almost in a car accident, about to get into a fistfight with someone, in the presence of some dangerous company or in a precarious or even potentially life-threatening position. My mom would say, "Larry, I felt that something was wrong!" Wow! That would always blow me away!

But this is not an unusual or unique thing that was only reserved for my mother. People experience this type of thing every day.

Thought replacement will help you to continue to stay on the cutting edge of your highest potential. The incredible possibilities that await the Real You will come to you as a series of breakthroughs that begin with changed thoughts, then a changed philosophy and a changed reality, which will always result in a changed life experience.

Trying to fix things from the outside is temporary and futile at best. But as you practice the right kind of thought exchange, you will see your purpose much more clearly; and greater strength, peace, persistence, faith and all of the other built-in gifts that have always been available on the inside of you will flow in your life.

We rise or fall to the level of our thoughts and words. As you are faithful to your daily thought replacement program, many of the wonderful things that you could not force to happen without changing your thoughts will unfold naturally. Instead of feeling as if you are trying to pull your dream-purpose towards you, you will know the reality of what it is like to have your dream-purpose pulling you forward to be who you were destined to be from your mother's womb.

Yes, there is a great plan for your life; and that sense that is inside of you, that awareness that won't let you settle for living on a lower level, is the voice of your purpose calling to you. If you want a better life, it will only be possible if you receive better thoughts. The quality of your thoughts will determine the quality of your life.

Chapter
7

Learning to Fly

I firmly believe that any man's finest hour— his greatest fulfillment to all he holds dear...is that moment when he has worked his heart out in a good cause and lies exhausted on the field of battle—victorious.

—VINCE LOMBARDI

You gain strength, courage and confidence by every experience in which you must stop and look fear in the face... you must do the things you think you cannot do.

—ELEANOR ROOSEVELT

Well, here we are at the last chapter of this book. If you read my last book or have ever heard me speak live or via a recording, then you already know I love eagles. Eagles are amazing creatures and tell us so much in paralleled truth about who we were meant to be. They have telescopic vision and can focus on the big picture as well as zoom in from a great height above the earth to see a fish swimming beneath the surface of the water. When a storm starts to brew, eagles cup their wings in a special way to catch the winds from the edge of the oncoming storm and then ride the fury of that turbulence until it drives them higher, where the sun is shining.

There are so many wonderful revelations that we can draw from an eagle's life that it would inevitably become a book in and of itself to even begin to scratch the surface of them. We will draw some more inspiration from this majestic creature with an eagle story at the end of this chapter; but, before we get to that, let's take a look at what you can expect to overcome and achieve as you apply to your life the words you have absorbed from the previous pages.

You are embarking on a journey of immense proportions. As you change your thoughts and pursue your dream-purpose as never before, you will be amazed at the heights to which you will be able to soar. You are an eternal being with unlimited possibilities. This is your heritage and birthright. The fact that you were purposed to pick up this book and that you have assimilated the principles and strategies laid before you is proof that this is your time. **The time has come to fire up the rocket of the Real You, fueled by renewed thoughts, and lift off for the next higher level of your purpose.**

You are blessed to see what you see right now. I am humbled every day by the fact that this message was opened up to me. As we see life more and more clearly for what it really is and how it really was planned to work, it makes us more grateful than ever to be here. We begin to realize that we have been given this beautiful gift called "life" and, as a packaged deal, we have also been bestowed with the wonderful gift called "our purpose for living."

Being grateful for life helps us to not take for granted one day in which we have been given these precious gifts of life, purpose, people and our dream. Let's make sure that we don't miss the very freedom and dream-purpose that are our reason for showing up on earth to begin with.

It's Already Yours—Don't Miss It!

There once was a thirty-two-year-old woman of little material means. She started out working as a housekeeper and a cook for a wealthy widowed lady. Over a period of time, her multimillionaire employer put more and more trust in her—to the extent that she was given unrestricted charge over every facet of the household affairs and also became her employer's closest confidante.

Ten years passed. The housekeeper was now forty-two and her friendly employer was now eighty-one. With the friendship and support that they shared, they became as close as any two sisters could be. The family bond that they shared helped them both avoid feelings of loneliness: they were both still single with no prospects of marriage.

Since the age of seventy-nine, the wealthy woman had spent hundreds of thousands of dollars on doctors and hospital stays, endeavoring to find a cure for a chronic illness that she was suffering with; but with each new treatment the relief that she gained was only temporary.

Finally, she knew that her days left were very few and she began to put her affairs in order. She was careful to ask forgiveness of all of those whom she felt that she had wronged in life and also gave generously to all of those who had been a blessing to her in business and in her personal life. For one person, she bought a car; for a teenaged young man, she set up a fund for his future college education; and for several others, she expressed similar benevolent acts of gratitude. The woman had no family to speak of, and the bloodlines that did exist had been disconnected from her for many years.

One night, she and her housekeeper were the only ones in the house and she called her long-time caregiver to her bedside. She spoke in a very low, almost inaudible tone to her trusted friend. With all of the strength that she could muster, she spoke these words in a weak and halting voice: "You have served me these many years, and I am grateful— not only for your labor, but even more for your loyalty and unconditional love that have always been a great source of comfort and strength to me. You have been my most loyal and trusted friend. Therefore, I am giving you this token of my appreciation."

With that, she reached over to the end table beside her bed and picked up a beautiful inscribed piece of parchment paper. An expert in calligraphy had obviously hand written it. The housekeeper instantly recognized it as the same elegant handwriting on the many certificates of appreciation that her employer had handed out at a gala affair at her beautiful mansion. This celebration had been held to mark the end of her ownership of the company that her former husband had left in her charge. At this farewell party, the elderly CEO had given beautifully framed, personalized and signed statements of her gratitude to all of the key people who had been the backbone of her enterprise.

The housekeeper's heart was touched by this gesture of appreciation and choked back a tear as she looked at the piece of parchment. Just then, her bedridden friend began to cough and gasp for air. Immediately, the housekeeper reached for an oxygen mask sitting beside the bed and carefully placed it over the ailing woman's mouth and nose. Within seconds, her breathing became more normalized.

A short time later, the nurse who had been hired to spend each night at her bedside arrived. The housekeeper looked at her watch and said, "Oh my goodness! I'm late. I'm going to miss my bus." With that, she left the house in a flash, rushing to the bus stop to catch the last ride home for the night.

As she sat on the bus, she began to cry, gasping every few moments to catch her breath. Though this attack of grief seemed to be an uncontrollable force, she still tried with all of her strength to muffle her sobs as to not disturb the other passengers. About halfway home, she pulled out the beautiful piece of parchment and gazed at it with mixed emotions of love and sadness while the tears fell from her eyes and caused the paper to begin to dimple. She carefully wiped the moisture off this valued memento; she knew that she would always cherish these priceless, heartfelt sentiments laid out as a masterpiece of calligraphic art.

After she arrived home, she went straight to her bedroom and, being exhausted from both the physical labor and the emotional weight of the day, she began to get ready for bed. While she was putting on her nightclothes, she glanced again at the piece of parchment, which was now lying on her dresser.

Just then she thought, "I wonder why my certificate of appreciation was not put into a beautiful frame like those that I saw presented at the banquet to the other employees." Immediately, she felt bad for thinking such a thought and, being positive, reassured herself that her employer would have taken the same care to frame her certificate except that she had very little strength and was confined to her bed. As she lay down on her bed to go to sleep, she said a prayer of thanks for the years that she had been privileged to be with her loving employer.

The next day, she arrived at work to find that during the night her friend had lapsed into a coma. Though the medical staff did everything possible to revive their patient, she remained in that state the entire day.

On the way home that night, the housekeeper stopped and bought a picture frame. As soon as she arrived home, she put the precious gift from her fading friend in the frame and hung it on her bedroom wall. Later that evening, she received a phone call informing her that her employer had passed away.

The next twenty-seven years were very hard and quite discouraging for this domestic servant. After her dear friend and employer died, she did not find as kind a person to work for. She went from job to job and never seemed to be able to escape the feeling that she was being looked down upon and mistreated.

At the early age of sixty-nine, the worn-out housekeeper had literally worked herself to death and lay in bed in her little two-room apartment knowing that she would probably never rise again. Her son, who was her only surviving relative, made a 1200-mile trip to be at her bedside.

He entered his mother's room, gave her a kiss on the forehead and chatted with her for a while, then went to the kitchen to get her a cup of tea. When he reentered the bedroom, the beautifully designed parchment piece on the wall caught his eye. He asked his mother, "Mom, what is this beautiful calligraphic writing that's hanging on your wall?"

She replied, "Oh, that is a certificate of appreciation from one of my past employers."

"What does it say?" he asked. With a mixture of aggravation at her son's forgetfulness and a little embarrassment, she said sharply, "Son, you know that I can't read. I started scrubbing floors at age twelve and have been doing that kind of work ever since. What use would I ever have for reading? I know that my employer expressed her gratitude, and that's enough for me."

"I'm going to read it. Do you want to know exactly what it says?" he asked.

"Sure, but I'm sure I already know the gist of it," she said in a mother-knows-best tone of voice. As he began to read those exquisitely penned words, he got weak in the knees and fell into a chair sitting beside the bed.

"Mother!" he exclaimed. "This is not a certificate of appreciation. This is a last will and testament. Whoever this lady was, she left you an inheritance of five million dollars!"

This sincere, hardworking little lady had been rich beyond her wildest dreams for twenty-seven years; she just hadn't known the truth about what was rightfully hers! She'd had the ticket to her freedom hanging on her bedroom wall all the time and never had the slightest hint of what was readily available to her.

Every individual on the planet was born rich. We are not just rich in the sense that we were born to experience financial freedom, which is one part of the total picture, but the full scope of this richness is meant to be an allencompassing freedom in every area of life.

This woman had been faithful to give of her energy and talent even beyond the point of proper regard for her physical well-being. Yet, she still never went the *extra mile* in her thought life. Oh yes, she was sincere, but sincerity and good intentions are not enough to really live your dream-purpose. The picture that she had of herself and the collection of thoughts that had created her philosophy and reality in life had sentenced her to an existence of hardship on a lower level than had actually been provided for her. The few missing thoughts that she didn't know in her "knower" were the keys to the critical mass that would have opened the door for her to begin to live a dream-life.

Yes, she was a multimillionaire and still *thought* that she was a pauper. What was easily within her grasp and rightfully hers was unknown to her. The absence of the truth of what really belonged to her caused her visions of freedom to remain only a fantasy. She had practiced *"the law of reciprocity"* by giving unbroken, loyal service to her employer-friend, but even working that one law faithfully had still left her reality skewed. She also thought she had to make it on her own and did not benefit as she could have by seeking out a mentor who could have had the insight to read for her the "handwriting on the wall," which was her true inheritance.

You Will Most Likely Become Who You Think You Are

I would be remiss to leave you on this valuable yet sobering note. We can cite just the opposite scenario in many life examples.

For example, Jack Robertson, who was born a paraplegic with no legs, came within 800 yards of swimming the English Channel.

Here is another great example. Ula, who was born into a home stricken with poverty yet she still, believed that she was born for freedom. Ula's husband divorced her and left her with several children to rear on her own with no support. She began selling slices of pie for ten cents apiece and worked various low-paying jobs until she finally saved up $1200 to put down on a piece of land. Throughout the remainder of her life, she amassed a veritable fortune from real estate sales and development. Before she died, she had donated over $100 million to charity.

We all have been inspired by the Mother Theresa's, the Gandhi's and the Nelson Mandela's of this world.

The thought that "it is impossible to live my dream-purpose," though a lie, will still become a self-fulfilling prophecy to those who meditate continually on it. But those who meditate day and night on the thought that "even though my circumstances look impossible right now, there must still be a way for me to break through into my dream-life" will open up ideas and strategies that would have never occurred to them otherwise.

There is a story about a guy named Charlie who has been hailed as "THE WORLD'S GREATEST BLIND GOLFER." One day Charlie was having a conversation with a renowned golf pro, and he proposed a challenge. Charlie challenged this U.S. Open Champ to an eighteen-hole game of golf with a bet of $1000 per hole.

The golf superstar responded in a sympathetic yet somewhat shocked tone, "Charlie, I could not do that to you. That would be like taking candy from a baby."

Charlie held his ground and said, "Don't worry about me. You just pick the golf course, and I will pick the time and date."

"Okay," replied the golf pro, "let's play at the Augusta course."

"Sounds great," said Charlie. "I will play you any night after 11:00 P.M."!

Yes, your thoughts determine what possibilities you can *see*, and *"what you see is what you get."*

I remember sitting in an audience watching a music group performing before thousands of people. After they were finished, a speaker got up and gave a talk. Those people on stage seemed bigger than life to me. I saw them as untouchable and their place of purpose in life as absolutely unreachable.

I'd had a vision of what I was going to do in serving my purpose years before while watching a speaker give a talk to a crowd of 65,000 people on a hillside in Mercer, Pennsylvania. But the years following that moment in time had been filled with a gradual blending in with the common-thinking people around me. I became more of a drone on an anthill with a feeling of insignificance when I looked at the larger picture of life. I was struggling along most of the time speaking for free, paying my own expenses and hoping to sell a few cassette tapes after I spoke in order to survive.

Then I hit that "wall" that we hear marathon runners talk about. Not only was there a "wall to hit," but you know from the parts of my story which I shared with you earlier in this book that there was also a "floor to sleep on" as well. At this low point in my life, I "got real." My deluding pretense, all of the mind games and excuses that I had been living with as my secret formula for evading my purpose, were thrown away. It was time for a decision to either break through that wall or build the wall higher.

Through the "inspiration of desperation," I chose to break it down so that I could break through. I remember that I had to work on myself every day just to keep feeling sane and to resist the temptation to give in to feelings of total despair. The daily thought replacement program that I used back then was a lot more hit-and-miss than the one I have given you in this book. But it still worked for me because I did the one thing that always wins when you are working with solid principles, even when your strategies are a little wobbly: the key that can unlock the door is called "daily consistency." I kept at thought replacement before I even knew what to call it, and I can clearly remember one of the times that I had a conscious shock that let me know that some kind of a big change had taken place in my heart and mind.

During that same sleeping-on-the-floor period of time, I went to hear a famous author give a speech. I had been greatly impacted by his books. His writings are probably among the top-ten best-selling books of all time. You can literally feel your life changing for the better as you read one of his works. This amazing person who has touched countless numbers of people through his life's message was a man named Og Mandino.

As I sat listening to him speak, I felt his message reach into a place in my heart where I had been desperately in search of direction. His friendly, loving and matter-of-fact approach to sharing principles was a style that you could tell was consistent with who he really was on the inside, and his heart even seemed to speak more clearly to me than his words. I could tell that he wasn't trying to impress anyone, and I totally identified with the realness of his message.

For the first time in many years I was totally sure, without a single doubt, that, though it would be with a different style of delivery, I was also purposed to share a message of genuine value with people around the world. For quite some time, I had "understood" what my purpose was; but at this point, I took a giant step forward in "knowing" the purpose that I am here to flow in.

What are your gifts and talents as they relate to your purpose? Your gift might be to share in the business world; to help people in their personal life physically, mentally, educationally or spiritually; or to provide individuals with some tangible product.

Raising wonderful children is definitely a powerful purpose in life, but what happens when they grow up and leave home? There is a gift that you are here to share that goes beyond the great care and nurturing that you provide for your family.

Whatever the main purpose and gift is that you are here to share, two absolute constants are the golden thread that runs through every human being's purpose. The first is that whatever your main purpose and gifts are, as you flow in them you are in some way blessing and serving other people. The second constant is that the activity of your purpose and gift is something that you could love to do seven days a week even if you never got paid to do it.

This, of course, does not mean there will not be challenges. And it certainly does not mean there will not be some parts of your purposeful activity that you love to operate in much more than other areas that you must attend to in order to effectively share your gifts and talents. But overall, you have to love the picture of your purpose from the big, wide strokes down to the fine-line details.

The accomplishment of the most menial task can bring some of the greatest fulfillment because you know that that seemingly small task is feeding the total life of your dream-purpose.

As I sat listening to Og Mandino, the voice of my purpose was speaking to me clearly and loudly—or I should say that I was finally in a place in my thoughts in which I could actually hear what was being said all along. An overwhelming sense of hope and fear welled up inside of me at the same time. On one hand, I felt a wonderful knowing that my future was secure as I continued to pursue my purpose with a passion. But on the other hand, I was stricken with fear when I rationalized that I had no idea how I would find the kind of opportunities necessary to launch me to the next level of purpose in life.

After the event was over, I was passing by the offices of the building where the seminar was being held. As I looked through the open door, I saw Og standing by a desk talking with the two men who were my mentors at that time. I walked into the office and greeted my mentors and then introduced myself to Mr. Mandino. Without any reservation, I blurted out the concern that was on my heart.

Speaking to the three men, I said, "Something happened to me tonight that is a little confusing."

"What's that?" one of my mentors asked.

"Well," I replied, "I had an overwhelming sense while Mr. Mandino was speaking that I was more 'on purpose' than I ever have been in the past, but at the same time my purpose seemed to scare me a little. I felt like I was not strong enough or sure how it would all come together. How can I get the same confidence that you guys have? How can I find the opportunities that I will need to go to my next higher level?"

Og looked at me with compassion. Without speaking a word, he seemed to say, "Young man, I remember being at the same exact place that you are at now."

Then one of my mentors put his hand on my shoulder. The hand-on-the-shoulder thing was part of his style. He would often do that when he was about to tell me something very important.

I thought, "Great. He is going to give me a step-by-step plan with the exact breakdown of A, B, C, D, on how to make this happen."

He looked me square in the eyes and said, "Larry, you will know."

That was it. I waited for the rest of the story, but it never came. I have to admit that I felt kind of ripped off. Though I tried not to show my disappointment, his answer seemed to do more to add to my questions than help to provide a solution.

I quickly said my good-byes and gave Og Mandino a warm handshake and thanked him for all the help he had given me through his books and his speech that night.

As I got in the car to drive home, my mind was perplexed and I kept saying to myself, "You will know? You will know? What kind of an answer was that? How does that help me with my present dilemma?"

After about twenty minutes of driving and fussing over my dissatisfaction with the answer "You will know," I said these words: **"I will know."** Then I said it again: **"I will know."** Then I said it accentuating the "I": **"I** will know." And then I said, "I **will** know." Then "I will **know**."

Then it hit me that the fear that I was experiencing was

fed not only by the fact that I didn't know how it was going to come together at that moment, but I also didn't believe that I was smart enough to figure it out and, therefore, that I would ever truly "know."

I remembered something that Og had said that night: "It is a great privilege to have been GIVEN the words to write in my books and to speak to you tonight."

I thought, "Wow...*to be given*. I didn't come up with this purpose on my own. It was given to me. And in the same way that I know this purpose was given to me, I also know that my purpose is real. And I can also know that the how-to steps I need to see my dream-purpose unfold will become clear as I move forward. **I will know the next step to take when I am ready to take it; and, in the same way that I know my purpose, I will come to know everything else that I need to know when I need to know it. "**

It was kind of funny, but once I believed that those words "*I will know*" were true, then I no longer needed to immediately know anything else! I knew that what I needed would be there for me when I needed it. Maybe it wouldn't get to me until one second before I needed it, but that was okay. My part in the process was to keep moving down the road of my dream-purpose so that I would arrive at the appointed intersections. At those intersections, the answers and everything and everybody that I needed to complete that phase of my purpose would be already waiting for me.

Wow! Did that ever take a load off my shoulders! I was so glad that my mentor had had the wisdom to stop at that three-word answer, "You will know." I believe that if he had given me a step-by-step outline I would have totally missed what my heart was hungry for. At that moment, I didn't need to know *how* it was all going to come together. He could teach me the action steps later. I just needed to know that the same dream-purpose that had propelled me forward thus far and had caused me to attract such great mentors would also cause me to be a magnet for all that I would need each and every step of the way.

I was thankful to be living my purpose and having the opportunity to do what I loved, which was my life's work of giving and sharing with others. I was struggling financially at that moment; but along with all the other "knowings" came the knowing that if I continued to be and do that which was my purpose, then the money was surely also waiting for me up the road at a future intersection. For now, I was supposed to enjoy the adventure and pass all the tests of changing my thoughts as quickly as possible so that my outer life would catch up to what I knew in my heart was my true destiny.

By replacing your thoughts and making your dreampurpose your world of reality, you become an authority on your reason for being here. You do not become an intellectual, brainy know-it-all; but in your heart, in the Real You, you become an authority. You walk, talk, act and think from the core of your being. You know that you know, and the people around you know that you know something. They may not know exactly what it is that you know, but they definitely know that you are onto something big. What they are picking up from you is that you are no longer in a state of wondering. You are now absolutely rooted in the authority of your purpose.

The Authority of Your Purpose

One day when I was in New York City for a speaking engagement, I decided to leave my hotel room to take a walk down Broadway. It was a beautiful spring day; and, though the New York City hotel rooms right off Broadway often cost three times what a hotel room would cost in the outskirts of the city, they are not necessarily three times as big; I was feeling a little cooped up. I was scheduled to give a speech at Avery Fisher Hall in Lincoln Center the next morning, and my hotel was right across from a little park. I did not have to do any business that day, so I figured that I would enjoy the sights of one of the "Big Apple's" most famous streets.

As I was taking my stroll, I stopped at a street-side vendor located at 53rd and Broadway to buy a bottle of water. Just then, I heard screeching tires and the loud sound of air brakes in full operation. Along with hundreds of other bystanders, I turned my head just in time to see a semitruck, with one of those long trailers on the back, laying strips of rubber on the pavement. The tires were vibrating with the pressure of the heavy load, and the cab of the truck bounced with sort of a skipping motion and turned slightly sideways. Then I looked directly in front of that huge semi, and there was a man who stood about 5'10" holding out his hand with a white glove on it. He was all decked out in the immediately recognizable uniform of a New York City police officer.

I looked at the size of the policeman compared to the size of the truck; and, though the driver of the semi never actually got out of the truck, I could see through the front windshield that he appeared to be a much larger man in physical stature than the traffic cop. The police officer could obviously never have physically stopped that truck and, except for the gun strapped to the officer's waist, he probably would not have been able to physically stop the man in the truck either. So why would he stand in the middle of a busy New York street in front of an approaching eighteen-wheeler and expect it to stop without even a dispute from the driver? Because he had the AUTHORITY to do so.

Why can you or I stand in the face of seemingly unbelievable challenges and still know that we are going to make it—and not just barely make it but break through and thrive? By practicing thought replacement on a daily basis, we establish a foundation of truth that sustains a strong knowing of the authority of our purpose. The authority of our purpose gives us the confidence to move forward with an awareness of our true destiny even though it may not yet be obviously visible in our present outer circumstances.

That police officer had received a collection of thoughts that had become his philosophy and his reality; therefore, he did not flinch in the face of a challenge. There was literally no doubt in his mind that when he reached out his hand, he had all of the authority he needed to command that truck driver to bring that rig to a screeching halt.

As you build your collection of true, principle-based thoughts on a daily basis, you will know with everincreasing clarity that you have absolute authority to go forth and make your dream-purpose a reality, even in the face of seemingly insurmountable odds.

Well, there you have it. You can unlock your better future, and your best dreams are now within your reach. In this little book, we have certainly not covered all of the "knowing and growing" that we will need to live our total dream-purpose. But we have uncovered and opened the doorway that *leads to* all that is needed to enter into the freedom to be and live our dream-purpose. It is the doorway to a renewed mind: a mind that is no longer cluttered with negative self-talk and blurred vision.

It's like the lady who constantly complained about how

dirty and dingy her neighbor's house was as she sneered at it from her kitchen window. One sunny day her face became flushed with embarrassment as she realized that it wasn't the neighbor's house that was dirty; it was her window that needed to be cleaned.

We are to be less intimidated by what people think and be more confident about what we know.

You have what it takes to go the *extra mile* in your thoughts, which will enable you to go the *extra mile* in your words, actions and deeds. We all have been given "what it takes"; it is just a matter of whether or not we will decide to "work with what really works."

Other people may try to make you feel peculiar, or they may be inspired to follow your lead and begin to renew their mind too. But what others do or don't do should become neither an essential encouragement nor a deterrent. No matter what others do or don't do, it is still our right to go *beyond common miles and common thinking*, becoming renewed in our mind and emotions, and to cause critical mass, which creates freedom. It is ours to have a mentor and be a mentor, to know the power of a daily thought replacement program and to learn how to fly to the heights of our purpose.

Fly, Baby, Fly

Until we meet again in the pages of my next book or perhaps in person at a live event where I am giving a presentation, let me leave you with this: a new eagle story. I encourage you to study the life of eagles, as I believe that you will also find many great parallels for growth and will also relate very closely with the flying eagle that you were born to be in the Real You.

One day, a mother eagle began to build her nest on a craggy ledge in a rocky cliff, high above the place where earthbound predators could ascend. She instinctively knew that she was soon going to be laying the eggs that would contain her little miracles of life. She gathered twigs to build the foundation of the nest, along with a lining for the surface that consisted of pieces of cloth, fur, feathers and grass. In the process of time, she laid her eggs and kept them warm with the heat from her body until she began to feel life stirring beneath her. Soon, her baby eaglets pecked their way through the shells of the eggs to greet their loving mother and their brand-new world.

Over a period of time, the eaglets noticed a pattern and a lifestyle developing through the actions of their mother. It consisted of breakfast, lunch and dinner in bed with extended playtimes in between. Though they had nothing else to compare it to, they thought the life they were living was pretty cool and that they really had it "made in the shade." They continually expressed their enjoyment of life and their love and approval to their mom via eaglet baby talk and continued to take full advantage of the seemingly permanent twenty-four-hour-a-day room service. "How could life possibly get any better than this?" they thought. "We like what you're doing, Momma. Keep it coming."

Then one day after one of her hunting expeditions, Mother Eagle returned to the nest and fed her babies. After they had finished their meal, she pulled all of the cloth, pieces of fur, feathers, grass and other soft, cushy materials from the surface of the nest and threw them over the side of the cliff to the ground below. The babies, with their limited experience of life, assumed that Mother was just remodeling the nest to make their little world even more enjoyable.

We can be very much like these baby eaglets in that we would often like to see every transition in life translate as a quick segue into greater comfort. If these were human children, one of them might have said, "What are you doing, Mom? Are you going to build a bigger playroom off to the side of the house? Can we get a Nintendo?"

But of course, Momma Eagle knew exactly what she was doing for her little darlings, and it had nothing to do with a more extreme level of instant comfort. After removing all of the soft padding that had lined the nest, all that was left were the sharp points of little twigs poking the baby eaglets in their bellies and sides, making them very uncomfortable.

A space in life where we are out of our "comfort zone" is a wonderful place to be, even though it usually does not feel great at that moment. Try this. Say the following sentence to yourself right now: *"Being uncomfortable can be wonderful!"* Notice how it feels when you say this statement. It usually feels quite unsettling and very affirming at the same time. We feel unsettled because we rarely enjoy the discomfort of stretching and growing through change. We feel affirmed because deep down in our hearts we know that we were not meant to live on the present lower level for the rest of our lives. This not only gives us hope for the future, but as we continue to know the truth about our purpose we also live with an awareness that whatever we are presently going through is ultimately working together for our good.

Well, these baby eaglets were getting more uncomfortable by the minute. When Momma Eagle saw that they had finally become thoroughly frustrated with the change in their living situation, she picked one of her babies up by the back of the neck and threw him over the side of the cliff. Down, down, down he began to plummet towards the ground, which was hundreds of feet below the safety of the nest. As the baby eaglet's fall began to pick up greater speed with each additional foot of travel, his heart continued to beat faster and faster until he felt it was going to explode right out of his chest. The baby eaglet's mind was racing as well, attempting to understand the situation. Though minutes before he had seen his mom as a wonderful, nurturing parent, he now began to question that assumption. "I thought my momma loved me. What did I ever do to deserve to be born into such an abusive home?" and a host of other contradictions shot rapidly through his thought process.

Just then, Mother Eagle swooped down; and, less than fifty feet from the baby's appointment with the inevitable, Momma swooped under her baby with amazingly confident precision and caught her little eaglet on her perfectly positioned right wing. She took her shaken "little bundle of joy" back up to the nest and gently dropped her baby back down into his familiar but unpadded comfort zone.

She then quickly grabbed another eaglet and tossed her off the cliff in the same fashion as the first. While infant number two was taking her fall, the first baby who had gone over the cliff called a meeting with his other remaining brothers and sisters.

Though it was a very short conference, there was an immediately unanimous vote in favor of a decision to call the Eaglet Abuse Hotline, 1-800-BAD-MOMS, and turn the mother in to the authorities. To justify their newly approved plan of action, the chairperson of the meeting plainly stated their case: "Our mother seemed okay for a while, but now she must already be tired of having kids and she's going to kill us off one by one." With stunned disbelief, the fragile little group affirmed that this was the overwhelmingly consistent perception throughout.

On a daily basis, this loving mother eagle repeated this seemingly irrational exercise of terror as many times as her little babies' hearts and nerves could endure. The eaglets realized that their mom wasn't necessarily going to let them hit the ground, but the possibility still existed that she was trying to scare them to death.

One day, as one of the babies was taking her routine, high-speed, daily jaunt, she once again passed each foot of space with an intense feeling of déjà vu. Then, all of a sudden, she was consciously shocked to realize that she was no longer taking a nosedive. She looked to her right side, then to her left, and saw her wings moving with a synchronized rhythm; and, though she lost the feeling of "being in the groove" every few seconds, she would quickly regain her posture and momentum in flight. With a great feeling of accomplishment, the baby eaglet let out a screechy call to her riveted sibling audience of "birds-eye-view" spectators: "I can do what my momma does! I can do what our momma does! I'm like Momma! I can fly! I can fly!"

Yes, life does present us with what seem to be less than desirable circumstances and even downright uncomfortable periods of change at times. We must know that this is all for our higher good.

Yesterday, as I boarded a jet to fly home from an Orlando, Florida, speaking engagement, I was once again reminded of the parallel between air travel and pursuing our dream-purpose. The pilot's voice resounded over the intercom speakers making an announcement that I have heard countless times: "Good evening, and welcome aboard. We have checked the conditions for our trip and wanted to let you know that before we reach our cruising altitude of thirty-seven thousand feet, we are probably going to be experiencing some turbulence during our climb up through the clouds. But once we reach our cruising altitude, we should have much smoother conditions as we continue our flight."

Once again as I heard those words, I thought to myself, "That is just like life." Just as we board a jet to fly from point A to point B and usually have to fly through some turbulence to get to the desired higher altitude for optimal fight, so we will experience similar turbulence in life as we pursue our dream-purpose. The thing to remember is that *the turbulence does not have the power to stop you or kill your dream-purpose. It is simply a doorway to your next higher level.*

When we decide once and for all that we will not be denied the highest level of our dream-purpose, then with total resolve we will volunteer to make whatever changes are necessary. We will do whatever it takes to not settle for less than the best that has our name on it. Positive thought replacement is a willing process that we choose for ourselves, not an obsessive chore to be endured. It is a life filled with anticipation of the unfolding possibilities before us.

We know there is no way to circumvent the irrefutable law that states, "As it is within, so it will be without." **If you can *know* it on the inside, then it is just a matter of time before you will *see* it manifested on the outside.**

Going after our dream-purpose in life can appear to be optional, and it is true that we can decide to evade it. But it is only possible to really be alive while you are living if you make life a great adventure and every day a continued quest for your higher levels.

Yes, *the magic is in the extra mile;* and that *extra mile* is filled with persistence, resolve, stick-ability, durability and a solid *"knowing"* that everything is working together for your good. These attributes do not come by trying to "beef up" our willpower through a mere exercise of the ego. One of the profound truths that we have observed throughout the pages of this book is that *"we are transformed by the renewing of our mind."* As this takes place within us, we ultimately experience through this change in thinking the result of a change in our *being* and *doing.*

Long after you have "flown through" the turbulence to get to the higher level of your dream-purpose and it is nothing more than a faded memory of a series of replaced thoughts, you will continue to enjoy the freedom of flying the heights of your destiny. **GO FORTH, AND** *BE* **YOUR ABSOLUTELY UNSTOPPABLE DREAM-PURPOSE.** *BE* **THE REAL YOU, WHICH IS AND ALWAYS WILL BE WHO YOU WERE BORN TO BE.**

About the Author

Larry DiAngi is living proof that the principles he shares will work if you "work them". He delivers keynote speeches and conducts seminars for both business and public audiences around the world. Larry is also the author of the book *The Resilient Power Of Purpose* (formerly titled: *How To Be Purpose Driven*) which is presently in its seventh printing.

During his early years it seemed unlikely that he would do anything significant in life. Then at age 17 he began a relentless study of individuals who had found purpose, meaning and success. This pursuit developed into a passion to share what he was learning with others.

His experiences in life and constant quest for principles that produce real results, prepared him to share these principles with people from all walks of life. From playing drums in rock bands, to shop work on an assembly line, then sold fire extinguishers door to door to businesses, a staff counselor at a home for juvenile delinquents, was sales director for a local magazine, then president of a corporation. For years he also hosted a weekly television show on an ABC affiliate and a daily radio program. Larry moved on to speak to audiences nationally and internationally as he has continued to do for the past twelve years. He has become a sought after resource for personal and professional development.

Larry's mission is to give people principles that will help them discover and live from the inspiration of their purpose, create breakthroughs, and go on to make their dreams a reality.